Prayer time between a fathe̶ writing about prayer from ̶ ̶ ̶ ̶ ̶ ̶ ̶ ̶ ̶ individual perspectives, Mark Driscoll and Ashley Chase have given us a unique look at how Jesus prayed and what it means for His followers today.

—JIMMY EVANS
FOUNDER AND CEO, MARRIAGETODAY

Prayer is one of the most crucial elements to us, as children of God, walking in an intimate relationship with our heavenly Father. And Jesus is our ultimate example of what real prayer looks like and how it brings us closer to the Father. That's why I'm so excited about *Pray Like Jesus*, a new book written by my good friend Mark Driscoll and his daughter Ashley Chase. Coming from different upbringings, they each offer their own unique perspective on prayer and how it's a simple, yet powerful, way to talk and connect with God.

—ROBERT MORRIS
SENIOR PASTOR, GATEWAY CHURCH
BEST-SELLING AUTHOR, *THE BLESSED LIFE, BEYOND BLESSED, AND TAKE THE DAY OFF*

Here's a book that actually explores prayer theologically and practically, a rare find indeed. And it does so in a way that will benefit anyone from the novice to the prayer warrior. Using the analogy of a godly relationship between a father and child, Mark and Ashley set the context of prayer. And then, using the prayers of Jesus, they reveal the practice and patterns of prayer that make praying like Jesus a reality instead of an unobtainable aspiration. This is a book that needs to be on your bookshelf or tablet.

—LARRY OSBORNE
AUTHOR AND PASTOR, NORTH COAST CHURCH

Pray Like Jesus is a book about how to have a meaningful prayer life, written by Pastor Mark Driscoll and his oldest daughter, Ashley. Pastor Mark and his daughter use their relationship as a model for how easy and uncomplicated our relationship with our heavenly Father can be. If prayer is an area you'd like to grow in, pick up this practical, relational, and life-changing teaching about the ways that Jesus prayed and how to get to know God as our Father.

—CRAIG GROESCHEL
PASTOR, LIFE.CHURCH
NEW YORK TIMES BEST-SELLING AUTHOR

Foundational. Encouraging. Helpful. Mark and his daughter Ashley's relevant perspective reminds us that our identity as children of God isn't achieved—it's received. It's a gift from our perfect heavenly Father, who desires to be in relationship with us. *Pray Like Jesus* challenges us to reframe our perception of prayer by providing connections and context of Jesus praying throughout the story of God. This message will help you posture your heart toward prayer and reclaim your identity as a fully loved child of God.

—LOUIE GIGLIO
PASTOR, PASSION CITY CHURCH
FOUNDER, PASSION CONFERENCES

The lovely combination of a father and daughter writing a book together has resulted in one of the sweetest, soundest, and yet simplest books you will ever read. The benefit is not only edifying reading but a sense of the presence of Jesus. What a testimony in our day of broken relationships that a father and daughter could produce such a book!

—DR. R. T. KENDALL
R. T. KENDALL MINISTRIES

I've been privileged to serve as a lead pastor for over three decades, but my greatest joy in life has been in being a husband to Judith, father to three sons, and now granddad to two tiny humans. Every other accomplishment in life and ministry pales in comparison. Therefore, I picked up *Pray Like Jesus* with a lot of interest. The beauty of this book rests not only in the revelation of God expressed by the authors but in their relationship with each other. Mark and Ashley use engaging stories interspersed with powerful truths from Scripture to reshape how we view prayer. You may think enough has been written about prayer, but Mark's and Ashley's unique perspectives on the topic and the engaging nature of this book make it more than worth a read.

—TERRY CRIST
LEAD PASTOR, HILLSONG PHOENIX

God is a good Father. Understanding this truth is liberating. Applying this truth in prayer is utterly life changing. Mark Driscoll and his oldest daughter, Ashley, lead us to see God the Father from the most reliable guide: Jesus. When we pray as Jesus prayed, life opens up and deep wounds are healed. *Pray Like Jesus* will take your prayer life to a completely new season of power and freedom.

—BRANDON THOMAS
FOUNDING AND SENIOR PASTOR, KEYSTONE CHURCH

Mark Driscoll is a huge gift to the church with a ministry that has touched the lives of millions, and I am thrilled to see that legacy expand through this book, written with his daughter Ashley. *Pray Like Jesus* is both insightful and practical in ways that will help you build a stronger, more vibrant prayer life. You won't want just one copy; you'll want to grab extra copies so that you can get them in the hands of everyone you know!

—JOHN LINDELL
LEAD PASTOR, JAMES RIVER CHURCH

It was a defining moment for us as parents. We were standing in my kitchen with Team Driscoll, circled in prayer, dedicating our new home to the Lord. Mark simply said, "Let's bless this home, kids." We bowed our heads. No awkward silence. No pulling teeth. One by one his kids jumped in with heartfelt, personal prayers over me and my family. I was deeply moved and resolved then and there to teach my young kids how to pray like that. This book is a biblical and practical overflow from a family that knows how to pray.

—PASTOR JOSH AND SHARON MCPHERSON
GRACE CITY CHURCH

I've never met a Christian who didn't struggle with prayer. We tend to wonder, "Am I doing it right? Am I praying often enough? Does God really care?" Even when you know the theological answers, it's hard to accept the practical implications. *Pray Like Jesus* is exactly what we need. It offers straightforward answers to our complex inner struggles. Pastor Mark and Ashley bring beautiful perspective and insight to this common area of angst. Prayer doesn't have to be hard. Just do it like Jesus! I wholeheartedly recommend this book!

—RYAN VISCONTI
LEAD PASTOR, GENERATION CHURCH

"Prayer is not something you *have* to do. Prayer is something you *get* to do." That is one of my favorite quotes from the Mark Driscoll and Ashley Chase book, *Pray Like Jesus*. It is an inspiring privilege to listen in on a father and his daughter discussing how to talk with the Father. The section on father wounds and how those hurts diminish our prayers was especially enlightening. Plus, the book offers solutions. This is a must-read not only for fathers but also for anyone who wants to take their prayer life to the next level. It is simple and brilliant.

—J. D. PEARRING
DIRECTOR, EXCEL LEADERSHIP NETWORK

Perhaps the greatest question among Christians today is "Why aren't my prayers being answered?" Mark Driscoll and Ashley Chase provide great assurance in this new book, helping the believer understand and recognize God's movement through prayer, and then trust His will as a result. The section detailing the "Who, What, How, When, and Where of Prayer" is especially helpful in building our relationship with the Spirit. Prayer is more than simply asking God for stuff; it is about trust and obedience. Mark and Ashley have given us a great picture of this direction!

—DALLAS BIVINS
PROFESSOR OF MINISTRY LEADERSHIP AND DIRECTOR,
GATEWAY SEMINARY, ARIZONA

My immediate response to *Pray Like Jesus* was delight to see a father-daughter book on prayer. My delight grew as I read the stories of their relationship and their very different lives as a backdrop for their book. It is both an expositional and a devotional book. The insights into the prayer life of Jesus and us as His followers are profoundly transforming. As you read and follow their lead, your prayer life will grow in likeness to that of Jesus.

—GERRY BRESHEARS, PhD
PROFESSOR OF THEOLOGY, WESTERN SEMINARY,
PORTLAND

Like healthy eating or exercise, prayer is one of those things we know we are supposed to do, but somehow we never seem to get around to it. What if we learned to see prayer differently? In their book Mark and his daughter Ashley remind us that prayer doesn't have to be just another obligation. It can be full of joy as we learn to talk to our Father, who loves us.

—GREG SURRATT
FOUNDING PASTOR, SEACOAST CHURCH

While many books on prayer look to Christ's example, *Pray Like Jesus* spotlights the relationship between our heavenly Father and His only Son. Mark Driscoll and his daughter Ashley Chase draw on their individual experiences as well as their roles as parent and child with compelling results. Their book will inspire you not only to pray more often but also to still your heart and listen for God's voice.

—CHRIS HODGES
SENIOR PASTOR, CHURCH OF THE HIGHLANDS
AUTHOR, *THE DANIEL DILEMMA* AND *OUT OF THE CAVE*

This father-and-daughter duo, Mark and Ashley, have written a guide to prayer that flows out of the closeness of their own relationship. It's a fresh and accessible word about God's children talking with their Father. It's practical, meaningful, and heartfelt. Don't miss out on their inspiring message.

—DRS. LES AND LESLIE PARROTT
#1 *NEW YORK TIMES* BEST-SELLING AUTHORS, *SAVING YOUR MARRIAGE BEFORE IT STARTS*

Prayer is the key to knowing God as our Father, our friend, our protector, and our provider. In a time when many people are living in fear, Mark and Ashley's book illustrates how we can live by faith. They show us how to build a relationship with God through prayer that allows us to overcome adversity and to triumph in life. I know they live this life personally. I've known the Driscoll family for years, and I love the way they work together to increase the impact of the kingdom of God on earth. They have built a wonderful church in Arizona and work tirelessly to share the good news of Jesus Christ. I'm thankful to know their family and see the fruitfulness of their lives. I recommend that you learn to *pray like Jesus* so you can follow in their footsteps of faith.

—MARK BUCKLEY
FOUNDING PASTOR, LIVING STREAMS CHURCH

What a blessing to see the power of the father-and-daughter team on such a life-changing topic—prayer! Teaching our kids to be prayer driven moves them to the next level of seeing and experiencing God's goodness in their lives. Read and apply and witness the transformation in our sons and daughters.

—Dr. Gregory L. Jantz
Founder, The Center—A Place of Hope

Prayer is what connects our heavenly Father's heart with our own, and while most Christians recognize they should pray, the practicals of how, what, where, and when can make a seemingly simple practice feel complicated and overwhelming. In *Pray Like Jesus*, Pastor Mark and his daughter Ashley show us a biblically based approach to prayer, presented through the beautiful lens of their own father-daughter relationship. Prayer is meant to connect us to the heart of the Father, and *Pray Like Jesus* will help show you the way.

—Jimmy Witcher
Senior Pastor, Trinity Fellowship Church

All too often we can take the idea of prayer and make it really complicated. In this unique book we see how our perception of God is often shaped by our view of human dads. Leveraging the dynamic of father and daughter, Mark and Ashley provide timeless wisdom that helps us connect with God and with one another. Along the way, they illustrate what a blessing it is to have a direct line of communication with our heavenly Father no matter what our relationship may look like with our earthly one. I've known Mark for years, and everything he writes is really good. So it doesn't come as a surprise that Ashley is an amazing author as well.

—Bil Cornelius
Lead Pastor, Church Unlimited

I've had the privilege of befriending Pastor Mark and seeing his family up close. He is an even better father than theologian. *Pray Like Jesus* combines the truth of Scripture with the tenderness of family. His oldest daughter coauthored the book, adding authenticity about praying to a Father of unfailing love. This book is a rare gift, showing with practical clarity how to approach the Father through the model of His Son, Jesus.

—MARK MOORE
TEACHING PASTOR, CHRIST'S CHURCH OF THE VALLEY

Pastor Mark Driscoll writes a very moving, personal, and practical book that will inspire us to consistently pray. We learn that we can approach the Father with the assurance that He loves us and enjoys fellowshipping with us the way He did with our Lord and Savior Jesus Christ.

—BISHOP JOSEPH MATTERA
MATTERA MINISTRIES INTERNATIONAL

Sadly most Christians have put prayer in the cupboard, bringing it out on special occasions such as family gatherings or when life moves into crisis. Mark Driscoll and Ashley Chase fantastically open the cupboard, dust off prayer, and help us discover a forgotten treasure that will become the centerpiece of our lives!

—LINN WINTERS
LEAD PASTOR, CORNERSTONE CHURCH

I have truly enjoyed reading *Pray Like Jesus*. As a pastor I have read dozens of books on prayer, and so many times you come away with a sense of your failure and shortcoming in this area of your life, but not with this book. I love the relational aspect that it emphasizes about our communion with our Father God. The teaching is solid and in no way condemning but saturated with the grace of God. The book gives insight into the prayers of Jesus, building a solid foundation for a life of prayer. Mark and Ashley do a great job of intertwining their relational aspect with our relationship with God our Father. A true life-giving book on prayer.

—CHRIS RICHARDS
SENIOR PASTOR, VINO NUEVO EL PASO

Pray like Jesus

BY **MARK DRISCOLL**
AND HIS DAUGHTER **ASHLEY CHASE**

CHARISMA
HOUSE

Most Charisma House Book Group products are available at special quantity discounts for bulk purchase for sales promotions, premiums, fund-raising, and educational needs. For details, call us at (407) 333-0600 or visit our website at www.charismahouse.com.

Pray Like Jesus by Mark Driscoll and Ashley Chase
Published by Charisma House
Charisma Media/Charisma House Book Group
600 Rinehart Road, Lake Mary, Florida 32746

of Tyndale House Publishers, Inc., Wheaton, IL 60189. All rights reserved.

Visit the author's website at realfaith.com, www.driscollbooks.com.

Library of Congress Cataloging-in-Publication Data:
An application to register this book for cataloging has been submitted to the Library of Congress.
International Standard Book Number: 978-1-62999-926-5
E-book ISBN: 978-1-62999-927-2

21 22 23 24 25 — 9 8 7 6 5 4 3 2 1
Printed in the United States of America

CONTENTS

PREFACE

THIS BOOK IS written by a dad and his oldest daughter about how prayer is the way God's children talk to their Dad. These unique perspectives come together to share life-changing teaching about the ways that Jesus prayed and how they help us get to know God as our Father.

As you read, you may find that you relate more to personal stories shared by Ashley—you grew up in an evangelical family and church, praying and learning the Bible from a young age. Or you may find that you relate more to Mark's stories—you did not grow up in an evangelical church and family praying and reading the Bible and met God sometime after childhood.

Before I (Mark) became a dad, I spent most of my life as a non-Christian. As a child, my Catholic parents took me to church and sent me to Catholic school for a few years, where I also assisted the priest with mass as an altar boy. I learned some ancient prayers from saints and memorized a few basic church creeds. I knew little about a personal relationship with God, how to hear from Him through the Spirit and Scripture, or speak to Him in prayer and worship. This lack of knowledge was not the fault of the church or its leaders. I just did not have much interest in spiritual things.

For me, everything changed as a freshman in college when I met Jesus Christ as my Lord and Savior. Suddenly the Holy Spirit gave me an intense desire to live a new life and learn God's Word. While I grew quickly in my faith, the one thing I struggled with was prayer. I did not know much about prayer, and I felt guilty for not being as devoted to prayer as the Bible studies and church services I attended were teaching me to be.

Philosophically I wondered why God needed me to ramble on in prayer if He already knew everything and had a plan for everyone. Emotionally, if I'm honest, it just kind of felt a bit odd to talk to God, kind of like the strange kid I grew up with who kept enthusiastically telling us about his invisible friend.

During college I married my high school sweetheart, but my prayer life was nowhere as consistent or committed as that of my new wife. Grace was a pastor's daughter, and she talked about prayer the same way a hyped-up winning coach talks during a postgame interview. For me, prayer was a bit like eating your vegetables—something you don't enjoy much but you do it because the experts say it's good for you.

Then something utterly changed me and my prayer life: in our mid-twenties, Grace and I had Ashley, our first of five children. When Ashley was born, my first thought was how happy I was. My second thought was how utterly uncertain I was about how exactly to raise a girl. I had been sure we were having a son, so my parenting plans for wrestling a lot and going to the dump to toss stuff out of my old Chevy truck were going to need some revision.

Thankfully Ashley grew up knowing the Lord as early as I can remember. The first time she read through the ESV Study Bible and notes by herself, she was eight. I've always had an extensive library of theological books, and around age eleven, Ashley started combing through the shelves. Before long, her bed was surrounded by stacks of books on apologetics to answer the questions her atheist friend was asking about most any and every topic of theology and genre of biblical literature.

Throughout her growing up and into the present, we are

often asked how we raised such a godly, strong (in a healthy way) young woman. My answer is always the same, "in many ways, her mom and I feel as if we watched the Holy Spirit raise Ashley."

One night, when Ashley was very little, I was undertaking our regular bedtime routine: worshipping together (despite my awful singing voice), cuddling, reading the Bible, catching up on the day, praying, and pressing the covers in around her, which we fondly called, "tucking her in like a burrito." As I prayed over her one night, the Holy Spirit showed up, and for the first time in my life, I finally understood prayer. With a big smile, she looked at me and said, "I am glad I have a daddy on earth and a Daddy in heaven who both love me. It's nice that I can talk to either of you anytime I want, and you will hear me and help me. Good night."

She smiled, closed her eyes, and went to sleep. For me, the Lord had just spoken through my little girl as He said He would, "You have taught children and infants to tell of your strength."[a]

As I walked out of her room and turned off her light, I felt as if God had used her words to turn on a light inside me through that sacred moment with my sweetie pie. Three things have stuck with my soul ever since:

1. God shared His title of Father, or Dad, with me. This revelation brought an entirely new, meaningful weight to my role. I wanted to make sure that as she, and later her siblings, heard about God the Father that my love for them as their earthly father did not cause them to be confused or scared of Him since we shared the same title.

---

a Psalm 8:2, NLT

2. My daughter knew how to pray very naturally. For her, it was talking with a Dad who loved her. This type of prayer seemed far more personal, intimate, warm, and natural than the more religious and rote way I had wrongly viewed prayer. It is also exactly how Jesus taught us to pray—something we will explore in great detail throughout this book.

3. Not only was I Ashley's dad, but I was also the Father's child. God was not only her Dad but also mine. If I wanted to grow in prayer, I needed to stop focusing on religious people and their ways of praying. I needed to start learning from my children as they brought their needs, fears, and joys to me as a dad who loved them and always had time for and interest in them. If my heart and mind could become more childlike, as Jesus taught, and focus more on getting to know my Dad than how to pray, odds are my prayer life would be more like my daughter's, which would be a good thing.

Ashley taught me a lot that day, and we're still learning together as we do ministry and get Bible teaching out about the Father's heart for all His sons and daughters.

I (Ashley) remember many nights when my parents would read me Bible stories and pray with me, and as I got older, I started to have a lot of questions and began to read and pray on my own. I thought that if God loves me just as much as He loves my parents, something they often told me, then He would certainly answer my questions and reveal Himself to me if I asked.

To me, age simply didn't feel like a defining factor in getting to know God and His Word, but since my parents had a huge head start, I wasn't ashamed that I didn't know much yet.

After reading through the Bible cover to cover for about six years in a row and thoroughly enjoying the discovery process, I felt as though a lot of my questions were answered, and I was pretty good at talking to God. I now realize that I had mostly just brought my requests to Him in very pointed, results-driven conversations. I could argue about answers to theological questions, but I had looked to the Bible mainly for inward knowledge, not relationship.

As I entered high school, my prayer life balanced out a bit thanks to the fact that I was leading Bible studies and sharing the gospel with others. These interactions required me to live out all that was in my head by building relationships with my classmates and having an outward focus in prayer instead of just making my requests. I would say that although I never had a crisis of faith at the level of doubting my salvation or walking away from the Lord, as a pastor's kid, I did have friends who asked me challenging questions that I took very seriously.

Many times, when I was wrestling with a friend's question that I just couldn't sort out, I would give up and tell them that I didn't know. Then, after a day or two, I would be journaling or talking to God about something else, and He would show me the answer. Through this process, He taught me how to listen, not just talk, and to be patient with His timing, something that I continued to learn during my senior year of high school.

During my senior year, my family decided to move to a different state right at the time I was deciding which college to attend. I wanted to be near them, but they weren't sure exactly where they'd be living. My dad and I were praying one night and both felt as though God wanted me to take a gap semester. If you haven't picked this up already, I like to accomplish a lot and move quickly (I wonder where I get it), so the idea of taking a break and "getting behind" after all the hard work I had done seemed silly. But God was right, and I'm glad my dad was there to help me confirm His calling.

I moved to Costa Rica for four months to attend a bilingual (Spanish and English) Bible school that focused on missions. There I had no cell service or Wi-Fi, so I learned to talk to and listen to God on a whole new level. I was completely out of my element—physically, relationally, and linguistically. I simply had to cling to God, the only consistent element of my life and the only familiar voice. I needed this time to mature before stepping into the next season of my life.

After my family settled in Arizona, I moved there and started to attend college, where I quickly got involved with various campus ministries, including a 24/7 prayer tent. I don't even remember exactly how I got involved, which I joke is how I know God wanted me there. Right in the middle of one of the largest universities in the country, we set up a prayer tent, where we sang worship songs, prayed, and evangelized twenty-four hours a day, seven days a week, pretty much whenever classes were in session. It was one of the great joys of my college years and taught me so many things about prayer that I will discuss later in this book.

It is an honor to be able to share stories of how God has used prayer to grow my faith and mold me as a believer. I love that prayer requires us to be dependent on God, much like a child who is helpless without a parent. God loves to bless His children, and since He is the only One who truly knows and can fill our needs, who better to go to in this often tumultuous life?

Those are our different journeys in a nutshell. Whether you find yourself relating more to one or the other of us, our prayer is that by the end of this book, you'll discover that you have a new perspective of your relationship with God. Once you know who your Dad is, it's a lot easier to talk to Him. So if you're ready to discover more about Him, let's get started.

Chapter 1

JESUS' SECRET TO PRAYER

Truly, I say to you, unless you turn and become like
children, you will never enter the kingdom of heaven.
—MATTHEW 18:3

Prayer.

Be honest. Does just reading that word make you feel at least a little bit guilty?

Talking about your prayer life often makes you feel scrutinized or nervous. It's the spiritual equivalent of talking about your diet or exercise—you know you could do better. You're easily embarrassed to talk about it or apologetic about your lack of consistency. Some don't know how to pray or don't pray enough; others only pray at the last minute, not unlike only dialing the police in the case of an emergency. We can't remember ever meeting anyone who thought they prayed often enough, earnestly enough, or faithfully enough.

Making matters worse, maybe you don't understand prayer, no one has ever told you how to pray, or, like with the kid in school who never really learned how to read, others just assume you know how to pray when you in fact do not and are a bit embarrassed to admit it.

We are here to help.

Prayer is not something you *have* to do. Prayer is something you *get* to do. Our goal is not to beat you up. Our goal is to

1

build you up. Talking with a Father who loves you and wants to hear from you should feel like a burden-lifting delight and not a burden-giving duty. Your Father loves you, always has time for you, likes to help you, and invites you, saying, "Call upon me and come and pray to me, and I will hear you."[a]

Grace and I (Mark) have five kids. One time when they were little, we were snuggled on the couch, eating popcorn and licorice while watching a television show about someone who had never met her dad. The kids were likely too young to remember that night, but I will never forget it. When she was very young, a child got separated from her parents while moving to America. The child grew up never knowing her parents and wondering whether she was unloved or abandoned. This loss in her life was a burden she carried into adulthood. As the now adult became a parent with her own child, she decided to finally do some research to hopefully discover who her parents were and whether they were alive.

> Prayer is not something you *have* to do. Prayer is something you *get* to do.

After some research, she discovered that her mother had passed away but her father was still alive. Amid a lot of internal emotional wrestling, she reached out to her father, unsure of how she would be received. The father was completely overjoyed and overcome with emotion when his lost child called. He immediately jumped on a plane and flew to meet his child, as he could not bear the thought of one more moment without her. The reunion scene had me crying so hard that the kids on the couch stopped watching the show and stared at me instead.

---

a Jeremiah 29:12

I was a hot mess, minus the hot. The picture of the father running with tears in his eyes to kiss and hug his long-lost daughter reminded me of the salvation experience for every Christian.

The father put his hands on the face of his lost child, who was now found. With tears running down his face and a smile on his lips, he said something like, "You wandered off, and I have been looking for you ever since. I love you so much! I missed you so much! I want you to tell me everything about you!"

Your Father God is like this. Your salvation is like this. In prayer you are a loved, lost-but-found child taking the time to talk with your Dad, who longs to listen.

In its most general sense, prayer simply means communicating with God, whether done audibly (as God hears our words) or silently (as God knows our thoughts). Prayer is the primary way we engage in a relationship with God, and just as communication is key to interpersonal relationships, it is vital to our relationship with God. Moreover, because communication is designed to run two ways, prayer can include both speaking *to* God and hearing *from* God.

When I (Ashley) started reading the Bible for myself, my dad explained to me that the Bible is God's Word, so praying to Him as you read it allows you to have a conversation with Him. This concept made a lot of sense to me, so I would pray before reading that God would teach me something new. Afterward, I would write what He showed me and thank Him. I have continued this practice to this day, and I still see Bible reading and prayer as inextricably connected.

I am thankful for this lesson because it came in handy while making the second-most important decision of my life: whom to marry. During my last year of college, I had a close friend who I was sensing was becoming more than that. He loved the Lord and served at our church, and my whole family loved him (which is a big deal when your dad is Mark Driscoll). I, however, was not ready to settle down, as I wanted to travel and work in South America for a few years.

I felt in my spirit as if I had reached a crossroads since my plans started to fall through, and I feared that, yet again, God's plan was very different from mine. Knowing this was a very serious decision, I began to pray and fast, and I even asked my parents and a few close friends to join me. I had some honest conversations with God about my fears and frustrations, and when I expressed my desires to Him, He graciously brought me to passages of Scripture that both convicted and opened my heart to see His way. Despite my emerging confidence in His plan, I knew I would need wise counsel to follow through, so I prayed that He would speak clearly to my parents as well.

As it turns out, my now husband was also fasting and praying at the same time, and after about a week, we talked and decided it was time to start dating. Our decision was confirmed by many things that God spoke to us audibly, through the Bible, and through wise counsel that all came together like puzzle pieces of God's greater plan—not to mention that we both felt a huge burden lifted after finally realizing God's calling.

A little over a year later, we are happily married, are serving the Lord together, and can see why God redirected both of our steps to His best plan, which neither of us could have imagined. As a Father, God loves marriage, and I was thrilled to have my dad officiate our ceremony at our church. And to top it all off, we went to South America for our honeymoon, proving that

God both has a sense of humor and wants to bless His kids so long as their desires are in His will.

As the Father's child, your conversations with God can be done anywhere and in a variety of ways, whether in a traditional posture of bent knees, bowed head, and clasped hands or in more natural ways, as when you're driving the car, mowing the yard, or shopping for groceries. You can journal your prayers or pray through the writing of songs or poetry. You can shout your prayers, or you can maintain a receptive silence, listening for the still, small voice of God. You can even use art and creativity as a way to pray.

I (Ashley) can remember doodling during my dad's sermons and drawing Bible verses on long road trips since I was very young. While living in Costa Rica, I began Bible journaling, which for me looks like creating watercolor art on the pages of my Bible when God brings images to mind while I read. I also paint while praying for people at times, as God gives me verses or pictures to share with them. Sometimes when I don't have the words to say, art helps me express what I'm feeling to God, whether it's a couple of scribbles or a complex painting.

No matter how or when you pray, the goal is always the same: to build your loving child-parent relationship with God. This concept has made more and more sense to me (Mark) as Grace and I parent our kids. One thing has remained constant from the time that our children were little to the present day, when I now look up at Ashley's three brothers, who have outgrown me: I did not much care what we did so long as they knew I loved them and we were building our relationship. When the boys were young, this meant a lot of wrestling, an infinite number of hours playing ball, and me frequently playing Goliath as they pretended to end my life in tribute to

David. When the two girls were young, this meant playing board games, having countless tea parties, and going on more than a few expensive daddy dates.

So long as they knew I loved them, we were together, and we were building our relationship, my joy came in seeing their joy. I wanted to be in their world, enjoying their company and capturing their heart. Not only did I love our kids, but I also liked them—and still do. God the Father is like that with you, His child, but He's infinitely better in a way that only a perfect Dad could be.

Big Lessons From Little Kids

Grace and I have always encouraged our kids to talk to us about anyone and anything. Often we could tell that they needed some help, advice, or comfort, but they were reticent to welcome us in to be close with them. So we'd lovingly wait until they opened up and invited us in. Sometimes we would respond by meeting a need. Other times we would work on getting their heart to change about something that confused or upset them. Much of the time, our goal was to get them to forgive someone and mend a strained relationship. Some of the time, their conversations with us moved our hand. All the time, our conversations with them were intended to move their heart.

God is our parent, and prayer is how we invite Him into our lives. Like any good observant parent, He knows what we are going through but often patiently waits for us to invite Him by initiating a conversation or taking Him up on His offer to meet with us. Sometimes prayer moves the hand of God. More often prayer changes our hearts as we capture something of

God's heart and are brought into agreement with and trust in Him. God doesn't need our prayers. *We* need our prayers.

We were created *by* God, in the image *of* God, to be in a relationship *with* God. Therefore, the primary purpose of prayer is nurturing and growing our relationship with our Father. Think of it like any happy and healthy parent-child relationship.

When is the last time you were around a little kid with a parent who loved them? How often did the kid come to check in, report what they were doing, ask a question, make a need known, seek comfort, report a problem, cry for help, or just be silly for no reason? How often did they assume that whatever they wanted to discuss with their parent was the priority and just walk right up and start talking no matter what else was happening?

You are God's child. Prayer is talking to your Dad. If you want to know what that looks like, don't worry about paying attention to religious folks with rituals, rugs, and rote. Instead, find some kids having fun with a loving parent, and do what they do.

The Bible is clear that adults have a responsibility to teach children. The Bible is also clear that adults have a lot they can learn from children. A few of the disciples once asked Jesus, "Who is the greatest in the kingdom of heaven?" (Anyone who says there's no such thing as a dumb question has not read about Jesus' disciples in the Bible.) Since they were standing in the presence of the Son of God in human flesh, the answer to this question should have been the guy whose mom was a virgin, who liked to water-ski without a boat, and who had the Father say from heaven, "This is My Son."

> *God doesn't need our prayers. We need our prayers.*

Rather than rebuking these Christian leaders for seeking greatness, Jesus surprisingly redirects them to true greatness. In the typical upside-down fashion of Jesus' kingdom, we read, "And calling to him a child, he put him in the midst of them and said, 'Truly, I say to you, unless you turn and become like children, you will never enter the kingdom of heaven.'"[b]

On another occasion, one of the most beloved scenes in the entire Bible, Jesus is a bit like Santa at the mall. Parents keep bringing their kids to sit on His lap to spend time and talk with Him. We read, "Now they were bringing even infants to him that he might touch them." The story gets off to a heart-warming start that every grandparent can relate to—until the way-too-serious ministry leaders show up and start acting like bad mall cops to run the kids off. "And when the disciples saw it, they rebuked them." The Christian leaders are a lot like us—they think that being with God is a serious business with no time for silly play and chitchat, which is why kids are to be out of sight and out of mind. "But Jesus called them to him, saying, 'Let the children come to me, and do not hinder them, for to such belongs the kingdom of God. Truly, I say to you, whoever does not receive the kingdom of God like a child shall not enter it.'"[c] This scene makes you wonder if *disciple* is the Greek word for *grinch*.

Kids have a lot to teach us. They have an innate trust and imagination, and when loved, they tend to open up and enjoy giving hugs, making friends, and making memories. Christian faith is not to be childish. Christian faith is to be childlike.

---

b Matthew 18:2–3
c Luke 18:15–17

OUR FATHER IS YOUNG, AND WE ARE OLD

As we get older, we tend to think of God as a cranky old man in the sky who points His finger, furrows His brow, and raises His voice. In return, we then think that to be godly is to be cranky. This mindset explains why the children never ran to the Pharisees and sat on their laps or played with them—they were cranky, grumpy, and irritable, not cheerful and fun like Jesus. It also explains why being with religious people is similar to being at the dentist minus the pain reliever to make it tolerable.

The truth is, God the Father is not a cranky old man. G. K. Chesterton said, "Because children have abounding

> Christian faith is not to be childish. Christian faith is to be childlike.

vitality, because they are in spirit fierce and free, therefore they want things repeated and unchanged. They always say, 'Do it again'; and the grown-up person does it again until he is nearly dead. For grown-up people are not strong enough to exult in monotony. But perhaps God is strong enough to exult in monotony. It is possible that God says every morning, 'Do it again' to the sun; and every evening, 'Do it again' to the moon. It may not be automatic necessity that makes all daisies alike; it may be that God makes every daisy separately, but has never got tired of making them. It may be that He has the eternal appetite of infancy; for we have sinned and grown old, and our Father is younger than we."[1]

God is not old; God is eternal. The difference is infinite. Baseball gloves, white bread, and today's pop music grow old, stiff, moldy, and outdated. God does not get old. God is not winding down like a grandpa or the car he drives. God is eternal and without sin, which means He is young, strong, and alive, unlike the rest of us worn-out and worn-down sinners.

Sometimes, when we pray to God, we feel as if we are bugging Him. We've all asked God the same thing over and over. When someone does this to us, we don't have the energy to endure it. So, we interrupt them, report that they are repeating themselves, and ask them to move on and not waste our time and energy telling the same story or asking the same questions. We do this because we have sinned and grown old. Maybe God is not like us. Perhaps God is more like a child. If you've spent any time with a child, you will quickly realize they have a remarkable capacity to do the same thing over and over—and enjoy it with fresh energy every time.

> God is not old;
> God is eternal.
> The difference is infinite.

When Ashley was little, she would have me (Mark) read the same Bible story to her every night for over a year. It was the story where a daddy named Jairus asked Jesus to heal his dead little girl. Rather than healing from a distance, as He did on other occasions, Jesus went to the bedside of the little girl, touched her, and brought her back from the dead so she and her loving dad could continue to enjoy life together. Every night, I would read at least one Bible story to Ashley. Then she would smile and tell me she also wanted to hear the story of the raising of Jairus' daughter. Each time I read it, she was equally excited about the ending, and she let me know every night how much she loved that story.

If I'm honest, somewhere around the one hundredth night in a row of reading the same story, I started to see my enthusiasm wane. We both knew the story, were well acquainted with the ending, but our responses were markedly different. Looking back, I think that my lovely little lady had more of the Father's heart than her father, who read her the story. Perhaps every time we bring the same sinful failure to be forgiven, the same painful memory to be healed, the same fearful circumstance to be calmed, or the same practical request we have made every day for a year, God the Father responds with the heart of a parent but the eyes of a child. Maybe each time, He experiences it with fresh energy, love, and concern. If He does not grow weary of hearing from us, we should not grow weary of speaking to Him.

We can learn a lot from kids if we have ears to hear and eyes to see. For example, when our kids were little, they each learned to ride a bike. Some picked it up rather naturally, others rather painfully. When first learning to ride a bike, the majority of kids have trouble figuring out what to do with their feet. Some kids jump on the bike and try to push both pedals at the same time, which never works. Eventually they learn to push one pedal down to build momentum, then push the other pedal down to continue building momentum, and then repeat the process over and over until they are making forward progress.

Learning to pray is much the same as learning to ride a bike. The two pedals are getting to know God as Father and then learning how to communicate with Him. People who don't enjoy a healthy relationship with God as Father find prayer to be as complicated, awkward, and imbalanced as trying to ride a bike with one pedal. The first and most important pedal to push down is receiving and returning the Father's love for you. Once that happens, prayer is as easy as pushing the second pedal on a bike ride.

Sadly many people struggle with the idea of God as Father

because they had no dad or a bad dad. Even people who had a good dad did not have a perfect dad, which can cause at least some confusion about relating to God as Father. We believe this is the biggest hindrance to prayer, and hope to help get this sort of debris off the road so you can start rolling forward in the next chapter.

REFLECTION

1. How would you explain your prayer life in the past and present?

2. What changes would you like to make in your prayer life in the future?

3. What observations come to mind when you think about relating to God the Father as kids who have a healthy and happy relationship with their dad?

4. Which person do you have the best conversations with? What lessons can you learn from that relationship about your relationship with God?

5. Is there any specific time in your life when you felt God was really with you in prayer and showed up in an amazing way to answer that prayer? Describe it.

Chapter 2

WHY WE MISS JESUS' SECRET TO PRAYER

For you did not receive the spirit of slavery to fall
back into fear, but you have received the Spirit of
adoption as sons, by whom we cry, "Abba! Father!"
—ROMANS 8:15

MANY YEARS AGO, in the early days of our first church plant, when both the church and Ashley were very small, in the middle of the sermon a young woman jumped to her feet. She stood there, shaking and frozen to her spot for a few moments before she turned and ran down the center aisle and out of the church building. Flinging open the doors, she made enough noise that everyone in the church noticed and was unsure what was happening.

Thankfully a few leaders followed her to see what was going on. Eventually she calmed down, her breathing returned to normal, and she was able to gather her composure and thoughts. She was not completely sure what had happened, but she had something like a panic attack because of the sermon. The topic was God the Father. Even though this poor woman loved the Lord, the word *father* was a trauma trigger. Upon hearing that word, she was taken back to years of abuse at the hands of a very evil father. In a demonic twist, the very name of God that was supposed to bring peace, comfort, and safety had become a terrifying title.

Sadly this woman is not alone. Over the years, we have met many men and women who report similar struggles with the concept of God as Father. These struggles vary from having some moderate trouble to major trauma.

HEALING THE FATHER WOUND

When you have something important to say, you usually save it for the end so that the odds are better that people will remember it. This explains why the preacher's conclusion, a dying loved one's final words, and the closing line of a politician's speech are usually the most important things said. As they say, we tend to "save the best for last."

As a Father talking to a family, what God would save as His closing statement of the Old Testament would have to carry the family of God for many generations. The weight of the closing of the Old Testament cannot be overstated.

The final words of the Old Testament are about John the Baptizer: "His preaching will turn the hearts of fathers to their children, and the hearts of children to their fathers. Otherwise I will come and strike the land with a curse."[a]

We tend to think of people in a variety of categories: gender, race, income level, education level, nationality, political party, age, marital status, and so on. God tends to think of people in two categories: those who are cursed and those who are blessed.

When we think of people being cursed, what most often comes to mind is witches casting spells, or Satan and demons

---

a Malachi 4:6, NLT

haunting, harassing, and hounding someone. Those things can be true, but what causes most cursing is fathers. God's final word was that families and nations are cursed for generations when fathers do not have a heart for their children, which in turn causes children not to have a heart for their fathers. The reason so many families are crumbling, along with churches and nations built on the family unit, is that a divided house falls just as Jesus predicted.[b]

Since we have three kinds of fathers, people can have three kinds of father wounds. These categories are not mutually exclusive, and someone can have multiple father wounds from multiple kinds of fathers.

First, we have physical fathers. We share genetic, physical connections with them and long to have a relationship with them and receive loving help from them.

Second, we have spiritual fathers. In addition to physical parents, the Bible teaches that we also have spiritual parents. This concept explains why we ought "not rebuke an older man but encourage him as you would a father" and to treat "older women as mothers."[c] Paul was a spiritual father himself, even though there is no indication that he had any biological children: "You do not have many fathers. For I became your father in Christ Jesus through the gospel."[d] Paul also refers to Timothy, Titus, and Onesimus as sons and calls the Christians in Galatia "my little children."[e] Peter calls Mark "my son."[f] Over and over in 1–2 John, John calls Christians God's

---

b Matthew 12:25
c 1 Timothy 5:1–2
d 1 Corinthians 4:15
e Galatians 4:19
f 1 Peter 5:13

children, as well as "my children," revealing the Father's heart in his heart.

Third, we have father figures. These are people in our lives that we wish would help us mature. Examples include coaches, teachers, stepfathers, grandfathers, uncles, big brothers, mentors, counselors, and so on.

Since no father is perfect, we are bound to have some degree of hurt and disappointment in one or more of these areas. For a moment, think of the most influential man or men in your life, whether he loomed large in his presence or absence, and ask yourself what he was/is like? Do any of these kinds of men sound familiar?

- **The missing-in-action man.** This kind of man died or was so sick that he was unable to function in a normal, healthy way. His absence was not a personal rejection but created a personal loss.

- **The deadbeat dad.** This man has walked out on your life and does little to nothing to help you, love you, or bless you because he does not much care to know you.

- **The addicted dad.** This man self-medicates with such things as drugs, alcohol, sex, porn, gambling, and so on. Addiction takes up so much of his life that there's no room left for anyone or anything else.

- **The Mr. Nice Guy.** This man is genuinely tender and kindhearted. He is loving, warm, and personable. He's not big on conflict or correction, which means he gets walked on a lot and has a hard time winning at work or defending his family from harm.

- **The selfish dad.** This man devotes his free time to his hobbies. He likes to hunt, fish, watch games, drink beer, golf, boat, off-road, or do something else with a buddy instead of his family. His time and money go to himself and his out-of-order priorities.

- **The party hearty pop.** This man is the nice guy who most everyone likes but hardly anyone respects. He is irresponsible, is unreliable, and loves to be the life of the party. You cannot count on him since he's immature and refuses to grow up and consistently take on adult responsibilities.

- **The domineering dad.** This guy is overbearing, is intimidating, and wins through bullying. Tactics include pushing you around physically, emotionally, spiritually, and mentally. These dads gravitate toward the military, sports, and the business world, where they succeed at ruling but lose at relationships at home.

- **The good dad.** This guy is not perfect, but he is present. He does care and tries to be a burden lifter instead of a burden giver for his family. When he's wrong, he apologizes, as he knows he is not perfect but wants to learn and grow to be a better dad.

I (Ashley) have spent years leading Bible studies and ministering to the various people God would bring to the prayer

tent on my college campus. I can confirm that all these categories of dads have profound effects on how young people—especially women—view themselves, their friendships, and their
romantic relationships, whether for good or bad.

Coming to terms with the fact that fathers influence our
lives no matter what kind of father they are is crucial in understanding how we communicate with our heavenly Father and
relate to those around us. When we don't deal with the flaws in
our relationships with our earthly fathers, we spend our whole
lives trying to avoid making the same mistakes in our relationships. But in the process we become so fixated on the issues
that we repeat them instead of finding healing from them in
prayer.

A father wound is simply an unhealed hurt from a physical
or spiritual father or father figure. Why does this matter?

First, we have entire theological and philosophical systems
built on our understanding, or misunderstanding, of God as
Father. Atheism denies there is a Father God. Agnosticism
says we may or may not have a Father God but that He lives far
away, He is not involved in our lives, and we will never get to
know Him. Deism says God the Father is a deadbeat dad who
lives far away, has nothing to do with our lives, and has no
desire for a relationship with us. Islam says their god, Allah, is
a father, but he is cruel, distant, controlling, not relational, and
a bit dangerous. Some liberal offshoots of Christianity think
God the Father is a passive parent who does not tell us what
to do, stays pretty much out of our lives, and approves whatever decisions we make. Feminist schools of thought are so fed
up with fathers that they prefer to worship "God" as mother,
including environmentalists who tell us to love the earth since
she's our mother.

The father wound explains these various misunderstandings of God the Father, as each is either a projection or rejection of a man on earth onto the Father in heaven. This thinking is completely backward. We are not to begin our understanding of God the Father by looking at men on earth and assuming He is like them. Instead, we are to look to God the Father and judge other men on earth by the character and conduct of our Father in heaven.

To heal the father wound, we need to forgive the father on earth who hurt us and start spending time with our Father in heaven, who can heal us. A father wound allows a failed earthly father to stand between you and your heavenly Father. Although He is there for you, you cannot see Him because your bitterness blocks your view. In this way, a wound is the spiritual equivalent of an eclipse where an earthly father blocks the light that shines on you from your heavenly Father. Forgiveness is how you release that man, remove that eclipse, and receive a new relationship with God as Father.

> To heal the father wound, we need to forgive the father on earth who hurt us and start spending time with our Father in heaven who can heal us.

All bitterness is a demonic stronghold that prevents Christian maturity from happening.[g] Regarding unforgiveness with a father, Jesus promised, "I will not leave you as orphans."[h] The orphan heart is the result of the father wound. Once you forgive your earthly father, your heart will be opened to receive the healing relationship you need with your heavenly Father.

---

g Ephesians 4:26–27, 30–32
h John 14:18

This is what the Bible means by calling God a "Father of the fatherless."[i]

On the cross one of Jesus' final seven words was "Why have you forsaken me?"[j] At that moment, Jesus took your place. At that moment, Jesus took on Himself all your sin and the Son of God was forsaken—or orphaned, as Jesus used the words interchangeably—so that the Father could adopt you into the Forever Family. Jesus Christ was orphaned so that you could be adopted by a Father who will never abandon you or orphan you. The most secure relationship in all eternity is between God the Father and you, His child.

It will not be surprising if in heaven the scenes of your life are replayed. You'll discover that when you felt alone and abandoned, God the Father was cheering from the seat that looked empty at your game or your graduation; He was putting an arm around you at the moment that it felt as if a torpedo hit the hull of your life. Living by faith instead of sight means believing that God is present even when we don't see it.

Second, since prayer is about building a loving, warm, healthy relationship with God the Father in conversation, it is impossible to have both a good prayer life and a father wound. This fact cannot be overstated.

LEARNING ABOUT THE FATHER FROM THE SON

Prayer is mainly about relationship. Prayer does include needs being met, burdens being lifted, questions being answered, hurts being healed, joys being shared, and fears being conquered. But all those things are in the context of a loving parent-child relationship between the Father and you.

---

i Psalm 68:5
j Matthew 27:46; Mark 15:34

The Old Testament talks a lot about fathers and includes genealogies listing generations of dads. God is referred to as Father roughly fifteen times, and those few occasions pertain to God's relationship with the nation of Israel, not warm and personal communication to an individual. Everything changes with the coming of Jesus Christ. Jesus' favorite title for God is Father.

A theological dictionary says, "The teaching of the Fatherhood of God takes a decided turn with Jesus, for 'Father' was his favorite term for addressing God. It appears on his lips some sixty-five times in the Synoptic Gospels and over one hundred times in John. The exact term Jesus used is still found three times in the New Testament (Mark 14:36; Rom 8:15–16; Gal 4:6) but elsewhere the Aramaic term Abba is translated by the Greek *pater*. ... The uniqueness of Jesus' teaching on this subject is evident for several reasons. For one, the rarity of this designation for God is striking. There is no evidence in pre-Christian Jewish literature that Jews addressed God as 'Abba.' A second unique feature about Jesus' use of Abba as a designation for God involves the intimacy of the term. *Abba* was a term little children used when they addressed their fathers. At one time it was thought that since children used this term to address their fathers the nearest equivalent would be the English term 'Daddy.' More recently, however, it has been pointed out that Abba was a term not only that small children used to address their fathers; it was also a term that older children and adults

> Living by faith instead of sight means believing that God is present even when we don't see it.

used. As a result it is best to understand Abba as the equivalent of 'Father' rather than 'Daddy.'"[1]

People who struggle with God as Father often have a great fondness for Jesus as if the Father were the mean one, the Son were the nice one, and the Spirit were the weird one. The entire concept of the Trinity is that God operates a bit like a family. The language of Father and Son, at the very least, uses the idea of a loving family to explain the relational nature of the one God who lives together as three persons in a loving, unified relationship. Theologians are fond of telling us that they each share all the same divine attributes and do everything together in perfect unity like a healthy family.

In a crowd you can often tell who the parent of a child is by noting the family resemblance. As the Son of God, Jesus Christ carries the Father's same character from heaven into the world. If you love and appreciate Jesus, the truth is that you are reacting to the character of the Father.

According to the Bible, when we look at Jesus, we see God the Father. Jesus said, "If you had known me, you would have known my Father also."[k] Jesus was then told, "Show us the Father."[l] Because the Father is invisible, immaterial, and spiritual, He cannot be seen as a human being in a body. It also explains why the Ten Commandments forbid seeking to depict God the Father with any physical reality or graven image. Just because the Father does not have a physical being does not mean that He cannot be seen. Jesus Christ took on Himself human flesh to enter human history, and in response to the request about seeing God the Father, Jesus said, "Whoever has seen me has seen the Father."[m]

k John 14:7
l John 14:8
m John 14:9

The entire Trinity works to get you into a loving relationship with God the Father. The Holy Spirit convicts you of sin, gives you a new nature, and opens up your soul to be born again and love Jesus. This explains why that same chapter, John 14, ends with fully half of its verses dedicated to Jesus' teaching about the ministry of the Holy Spirit. In short, the Holy Spirit brings you to Jesus Christ, the Son of God. The Son of God then brings you to God the Father.

In the middle of this same discussion about getting to God the Father, Jesus summarized His entire earthly mission, saying, "I am the way, and the truth, and the life. No one comes to the Father except through me."[n] Lots of Christians have received the Spirit and met Jesus but still not made the final step of their spiritual walk into a warm, loving relationship with God as Father. These people are filled with the Spirit and love Jesus but are still not fully healed because they have a remaining father wound manifested as an "orphan" spirit.[o] Once you begin to experience a healthy relationship with the Father, not only will you start to grow in health, but also your prayer life will naturally and continually improve. People in a relationship talk to one another to build their relationship. Until you have a relationship, communication simply cannot exist.

Getting to know and trust God as Father starts by looking at Jesus the Son. When the Bible says that people, including Jesus, are God's image bearers, it means that people are made to mirror. The job of the mirror in your bathroom and car are simple—to accurately reflect your image. A mirror does not exist to create images but only to reflect. This concept is

---

n John 14:6
o John 14:18

precisely what the Bible means, saying that Jesus "is the image of the invisible God,"[p] All that you see and appreciate in Jesus is a perfect reflection of the Father heart of God, which should invite you to pray to God as Father, as Jesus did.

OUR FATHER

Jesus prays, "Abba, Father, all things are possible for you.... Yet not what I will, but what you will."[q]

This prayer shows us both Jesus' relational intimacy with God (calling him Abba) and his submission to the Father's authority and will. In this example, we learn two things: prayer to the Father should always be respectful but need not be formal.

I (Mark) grew up in a religious tradition where the prayers were very memorized, very ritualized, very formalized. And this trains us to think we have to jump through certain religious hoops to get our prayers heard.

As I (Ashley) was growing up, we had some traditions around prayer, such as praying at dinner and before bed, but this was mainly to build good habits, and these were not the only times we prayed. Telling God what we were thankful for around the dinner table was always a highlight for me and is something my husband and I still do to this day. Praying before bed was a way for my parents to bless us and model prayer so that we could learn to participate. But beyond that I remember my parents praying for what seemed to me like little things, such as that we'd drive somewhere safely, to big things, such as that God would provide us with a church building.

We kept a journal of many requests and one by one would cross them off as God chose to answer them. Sometimes the

p Colossians 1:15
q Mark 14:36

prayers were short and simple and took place in the middle of the grocery store, and sometimes they were long and thought out in private. It all depended on the person or need for which we were praying.

God is a loving Father who loves to hear from His children. He welcomes your prayers: "For you did not receive the spirit of slavery to fall back into fear, but you have received the Spirit of adoption as sons, by whom we cry, 'Abba! Father!'"[r]

Adults can learn a lot about prayer by hanging out with children. For example, at the age of six, one of my five children wanted to go swimming. He didn't approach me (Mark), saying, "Dearest Father, despite the horror of my sin and unworthy fallen nature, I beseech thou to swimmeth with me." He just said, "Dad, can we go swimming?" He didn't hem and haw; he didn't have to make a fifteen-minute speech; he didn't have to be uptight. He did not need to quote dead theologians. He knows that I love him and that he has the freedom to ask me for things. I love my son; he's my boy! All he has to do is ask.

Some of us are just way too serious with our prayers. This doesn't mean that prayer isn't a serious business; it just means that too many of us think that if we pray in specific ways and with certain speech, God will be more inclined to hear us. But God is our Abba Father, our Dad. He wants to listen to us, answer us, and help us. He doesn't require any more formalized rituals than any other loving dad would. We don't have to be uptight about prayer.

Because of this the Bible says we can approach the throne of grace boldly![s] Our Father loves us and wants to hear from us. Dad cares. He's available; we just need to talk to Him.

---

r Romans 8:15
s Hebrews 4:16

We also need to remember that prayer is not telling God something He doesn't already know. You can't surprise God!

In meeting with people with various issues, we often ask, "Well, have you talked to God about this?" and it is remarkable how often some say, "Oh, no, I could never talk to God about this!" There's no information you have that God doesn't already know; your telling Him something will never put Him in the know. You're not going to shock God or catch Him off guard.

To me (Ashley) and many people I have known, this is an incredibly comforting fact. I once shared the gospel with a girl who felt that she couldn't tell God what she had done or what had been done to her, and she hadn't even told her best friend or parents due to overwhelming shame. She knew the situation wasn't entirely her fault, but she felt so blameworthy that she kept it to herself and was emotionally crippled in fear of someone finding out. I gently explained to her that God already knew about everything she was holding inside and He wanted to heal her if she would let him.

She started bawling in disbelief that God didn't want to punish her or look at her as damaged goods. But she also struggled to understand why God didn't prevent her from being harmed in the first place, which I later discovered was partially due to her irresponsible dad, who didn't protect her or impart much wisdom about men. She allowed me to pray for her at that moment and slowly opened up to the idea of praying on her own the more we got to know each other and were able to separate her earthly experiences from her view of the heavenly Father.

My kids often tell me (Mark) things that I already know, but their telling me is about talking to me, experiencing relational intimacy with me, and inviting me in to be with them. It's about the experience of me loving them, serving them, helping them, instructing them, and caring for them. Conversation is key to all relationships.

When you have a problem or a concern, take it to God and talk about it with Him, just as Jesus did. While there are times when we pray to God the Son (as Stephen did at his death in Acts 7:59) or to the Holy Spirit, ideally prayer is Trinitarian.

Most times, we pray *to* the Father, *through* the Son, *by* the presence and the power of the indwelling Holy Spirit. Our prayers as Christians exemplify our participation in the life of the Trinity. This concept matters greatly because if we do not understand who God is, then we cannot understand who we are. These are perhaps the two most important first

> Most times, we pray *to* the Father, *through* the Son, *by* the presence and the power of the indwelling Holy Spirit.

things we need to know rightly—who God is and who God says we are. Once these two truths are straight, the rest of life can be straightened out.

Sadly, many Bible-believing, Jesus-loving, Spirit-following Christians get these two things wrong.

IS GOD YOUR FATHER OR MASTER? ARE YOU HIS SON OR SLAVE?

When Ashley was first born, her mother and I held her, prayed for her, and kept telling her that we were her parents. Instinctively we knew that she needed to know who we were and that we were there to love her, protect her, and provide for her.

What is true when we are born is also true when we are born again. The first thing we need to know is who our parent is: "Because you are sons, God has sent the Spirit of his Son into our hearts, crying, 'Abba! Father!' So you are no longer a slave, but a son, and if a son, then an heir through God."[t] The story line of the Bible is that we are born as "slaves of sin"[u] and "by nature children of wrath."[v] Simply stated, we were born with Satan as our father, the same as the religious leaders Jesus rebuked,[w] and we are enslaved by sin and death. When the Holy Spirit gave you a new heart and made you a new person, He also gave you a new Father and new freedom from sin.

Do you relate to God as master or Father?

Many Christians struggle to relate to God as Father because they mistakenly see Him as master. Just as the children of Israel were no longer slaves when God freed them from Egyptian bondage, they still had a slave mindset that struggled to live in freedom and the love of God the Father, even longing to go back to their old way of life under a master as slaves. The difference between seeing God as master and Father is profound and affects every aspect of your relationship with God, particularly prayer.

GOD AS MASTER vs. GOD AS FATHER	
A master uses you	A father blesses you
You serve a master	A father serves you
A master motivates you by fear	A father motivates you by love
A master beats you down	A father builds you up
No grace for an inheritance	Full grace for an inheritance

t Galatians 4:6–7
u Romans 6:17
v Ephesians 2:3
w John 8:44

Many people struggle with prayer because they wrongly view God as master. If God is mean, unloving, controlling, and harsh and uses you, then running to Him to build a loving, intimate relationship by inviting Him into every aspect of your life is the very last thing you would do. Conversely, if God is your Father, that is the *very* thing you should do.

I (Ashley) have known many young people to be so passionate about their faith and doing the right thing that they go to great lengths to keep a rigorous schedule of prayer, fasting, Bible reading, and other externally visible spiritual disciplines. They are often honored for their dedication and devotion, mainly because they let everyone know exactly how dedicated

> The difference between seeing God as master and Father is profound and affects every aspect of your relationship with God, particularly prayer.

they are. But whenever they miss a scheduled time with the Father or He doesn't "show up," they fear He could be angry or disappointed with them. Or perhaps even worse, they judge others for not being as devoted as they are. Our God is not a god who must be won over by sacrifices and outward actions as much as He is a Father who wants to spend time with His kids.

On occasion I would talk about these religious zealots to classmates who didn't know Jesus, and they saw no benefit in becoming part of what they saw represented as Christianity, no matter how hard anyone tried to convince them or scare them into it. In one instance, these zealots even told me that I might not be saved because I didn't follow the rules of a specific group! With both the religious and rebellious, I've found that pointing them to Jesus' relationship with the Father in the Gospels is the only way to learn the truth about what the Father requires of us. Our prayer lives should look like His prayer life.

Do you see yourself as a slave or a son?

A son or daughter with a father lives *from* their identity. Conversely, a slave with a master lives *for* their identity. If they perform well and please the master, they are rewarded. If they fail to perform well for the master, they are punished. A slave has to earn their identity and can lose it at any time. This reality causes great pressure to perform, be perfect, and not disappoint in any way.

Many people—especially if they had a perfectionist, religious, demanding, military-minded, or competitive parent—are hardwired to believe in a works-based identity. A works-based identity is earned and can be lost. The opposite is a grace-based identity, which is not *achieved* by you but *received* by you as a gift from the Father given by your big brother Jesus that cannot be lost.

Satan is the "father of lies,"[x] and one of his most persistent, pernicious, and perilous lies is telling us that our identity is not secure in the Father's love for us.

Consider Jesus Christ, the Son of God. Having spent the first roughly thirty years of His life obeying His parents as a kid and working a carpentry job with His earthly father as a young man, Jesus began His public ministry by being baptized. Before Jesus had seemingly preached a sermon, healed the sick, or performed a miracle, God the Father spoke from heaven, saying, "You are my beloved Son; with you I am well pleased."[y]

---

x John 8:44
y Luke 3:22

In the very next chapter, Satan shows up and says two times, "If you are the Son of God," then you need to prove and achieve it by doing something.[z] Jesus, by faith, believed who the Father said He was as Son, lived from that identity, and walked in spiritual victory.

When you know that God is your Father and you are His child, God's love floods your life from heaven. When you do not know or fail to believe these two truths, hell comes up to burn down your life.

As a dad, no matter what our kids do, I am still their dad, who loves them, who wants to be a blessing to their lives, and who lifts burdens. "When we were children, were enslaved to the elementary principles of the world...God sent forth his Son...so that we might receive adoption as sons."[aa]

Those who see God as master tend to see themselves as slaves. Those who see God as Father tend to see themselves as sons and daughters.

SLAVE vs. SON	
Controlling relationship	Loving relationship
Powerless	Empowered
Works-based lifestyle	Grace-based lifestyle
Forever out of the family	Forever in the family

In the ancient world, upwards of half of the Roman Empire was slaves. They were regarded as property, had little to no legal rights, were treated as machines and beasts worked to death, and were not allowed to be part of the family or receive any of the family inheritance. Sons, however, were loved as heirs, had legal rights, were treated with love, were included

z   Luke 4:3, 9
aa   Galatians 4:3–5

in the family, and received a full inheritance. This difference is why God the Father tells us that we are "sons of God," with both sons and daughters receiving the same full legal status as was given the sons in the ancient world.

If God is your master and you are His slave, you will not have much of a relationship or spend any significant amount of time inviting Him into the deepest details of your life. If God is your Father and you are His son or daughter, everything changes and prayer happens as easily as a conversation between a loved, secure child and a parent who is for them and always there for them.

I (Ashley) have seen many people who view God as a slave driver eventually give up on trying to have a relationship with Him altogether since it seems as if even when they do the right things, He doesn't seem to notice or care. And when they pray, He doesn't seem to listen. They grow weary and go back to their sinful habits because following God doesn't seem to add much value to their daily lives yet requires a lot of effort.

These are all lies that Satan tells to keep us enslaved to sin instead of truly being free. God often doesn't answer prayer exactly when or how we ask, but the more we get to know Him, the more our hearts are aligned with His and the more we hear His voice more clearly above all the noise that the enemy throws at us. Carefully studying His Word and being devoted to prayer teach us who He is and who we are in relation to Him, which helps us to be aware of what He is doing around us.

DEAR DADS

Let me (Mark) say to every dad reading this chapter, the person most likely to curse your family for generations is you. Women and demons can be problems, but the biggest problem is usually the dad. Because of this, Jesus told some men, "You are of your father the devil, and your will is to do your father's desires."[ab] The adage "Like father, like son" rings true, and the devil's boys look a lot like their dad. Make no mistake, the majority of our social problems would be solved by dads living, loving, and leading with the Father heart of God. The single greatest cure for poverty, crime, and

> The single greatest cure for poverty, crime, and moral decay is the presence of fathers with the Father heart of God.

moral decay is the presence of fathers with the Father heart of God. More than additional cops, prisons, and government, kids need good, godly dads.

Just as cursing flows down from those in leadership because they are the head, so does blessing. If a father becomes a Christian and gets a new heart by the Spirit, a new life by the Son, and a new relationship with the Father, the blessings of God fall *on* that man and fall *through* that man to his family for generations.

Once people become children of God, they then learn to parent their kids the way God parents them. Too often it is the single mom raising the kids or the married mom taking the kids to church and teaching the kids about Jesus without the dad's involvement. Women and children are more likely to attend church, read the Bible, pray, and tithe than men statistically. Men are missing a massive opportunity to have the Father's blessing reign down on them, in them, and through them to their families. If your wife or child gives you this book,

---

ab John 8:44

men, it is because the Father wants to do something powerful through you so that generations can be blessed.

At the end of Genesis, a family of around seventy people moved to Egypt. Some four hundred years later, that same family left as a nation of a few million to establish Israel as the world headquarters for mission and ministry, awaiting the coming of Jesus Christ! Too often men think far more about having a good time than they think about leaving a good legacy. In four hundred years, how many of your descendants will be alive, and will they be cursed or blessed?

> Too often men think far more about having a good time than they think about leaving a good legacy.

It is rightly said,

One man can make a difference. Churchill saved England. Lombardi turned the Packers from doormats into legends. Namath convinced the Jets they could win the [national football championship]. Iacocca turned Chrysler around. It happens all the time. One man can make a difference. Jonathan Edwards was one man who made a difference. Born in 1703, he was perhaps the most brilliant mind America ever produced. A pastor, writer, and later, president of Princeton, he and his wife had eleven children. Of his known male descendants:

- More than three hundred became pastors, missionaries, or theological professors.

- 120 were professors at various universities.

- 110 became attorneys.

- Sixty were prominent authors.

- Thirty were judges.

- Fourteen served as presidents of universities and colleges.

- Three served in the U.S. Congress.

- One became vice president of the United States.[2]

In addition to the life we live, there is a legacy we leave. Jonathan Edwards lived an amazing life as arguably the greatest theologian in the history of America, but his legacy is even greater than his life. He was a devoted dad whose descendants have been world changers.

> Jesus' teaching that God is our Father combined with Paul's teaching that we are His sons completely transforms what it means for a man to have a loving relationship with God.

The secret to Edwards' powerful legacy was his prayerful life:

> He began the day with private prayers followed by family prayers, by candlelight in the winter. Each meal was accompanied by household devotions, and at the end of each day Sarah joined him in his study for prayers. Jonathan kept secret the rest of his daily devotional routine, following Jesus' command to pray in secret. Throughout the day, his goal was to remain constantly with a sense of living in the presence of God, as difficult as that might be. Often he added secret days of fasting and additional prayers.[3]

I know that for many men, prayer can be hard because it involves communication and emotion—two things that many men do not consider manly. Jesus is the perfect man, and

He prayed emotional prayers. Jesus' teaching that God is our Father, combined with Paul's teaching that we are His sons, completely transforms what it means for a man to have a loving relationship with God.

Furthermore, men become like their view of God the Father and treat their kids the way they see God treat them. Until men get a healthy view of God as Father and of themselves as sons, not only does their relationship with God suffer but so does their relationship with their children. To learn how to pray like God's kids to our heavenly Father, we will examine the prayer life of Jesus Christ, the Son of God, starting in the next chapter.

REFLECTION

1. a. What is your relationship with your physical father(s) like? What category would you put him in (missing-in-action, deadbeat, addicted, Mr. Nice Guy, selfish, party hearty, domineering, good)? How does this relationship affect your prayers to the heavenly Father?

1. b. What is your relationship with your spiritual father(s) like? What category would you put him in (missing-in-action, deadbeat, addicted, Mr. Nice Guy, selfish, party hearty, domineering, good)? How does this relationship affect your prayers to the heavenly Father?

1. c. What is your relationship with your father figure(s)? What category would you put him in (missing-in-action, deadbeat, addicted, Mr. Nice

Guy, selfish, party hearty, domineering, good)? How does this relationship affect your prayers to the heavenly Father?

2. Has God revealed any father wounds in your life? If so, list them and begin to process them with the Father.

3. What has Jesus taught you about prayer?

4. Do you view God as Father or master? Do you see yourself as a son or a slave? How do these views affect your prayers?

5. If you are a dad, how can you grow in your prayer life? Why is it important for you to set an example for your family?

Chapter 3

PRAY LIKE JESUS

Lord, teach us to pray.
—Luke 11:1

EVER SINCE I (Ashley) was little, I remember God placing a desire in my heart to learn Spanish. I had some amazing elementary schoolteachers that encouraged my excitement for the language, and as I got older, I felt that for some reason God had wired my brain for language learning.

In high school I started volunteering with a program that taught English to Spanish-speaking moms in my community and even started going on mission trips to Spanish-speaking countries. I felt God calling me to minister to Spanish speakers, so I was even more motivated to keep studying and practicing. This calling led me to attend Bible college in Costa Rica after high school to learn to study the Bible in Spanish and effectively share the gospel.

As a kindergartner, I had no idea that God wanted me to learn Spanish so that I could tell people about Jesus in Mexico and Costa Rica and beyond. I had no idea that I would eventually teach English to Spanish-speaking immigrants in Arizona and help them get jobs so their families could be stable. Or that I would help translate my dad's books into Spanish so that more of the world could hear the good news. I simply thought it was fun, and since I was young, I didn't feel bad that it took me so long to learn and was incredibly challenging at times, especially since I'm still learning daily!

Learning to pray is similar to learning a new language. You simply have to start somewhere, even if it seems as if it is a steep learning curve or you feel behind everyone else. Maybe you have zero motivation to learn a language and don't feel as if you ever could succeed in it. Thankfully our motivation to learn to pray should be to communicate with our Father, and He's given us everything we need to do so in His Word and through the Holy Spirit.

PRAYING BY THE SPIRIT

When children are little, they have to learn everything. They do not come into the world knowing how to say a word, drink out of a cup, or tie their shoes. So children end up asking their parents a lot of questions.

When we are born again as God's children, this process repeats itself. We do not instantly know the Bible or how to pray and worship when we are born again. These are things that we must learn, so we need to ask God a lot of questions to help us.

This process happened a lot in the Bible. One example is when the disciples said to Jesus, "Lord, teach us to pray."[a] Jesus responded that if they, who were sinful, still knew how to give good things to their children, how much more would the Father in heaven give the Holy Spirit to anyone who asked Him.[b]

a Luke 11:1
b Luke 11:13

Jesus was teaching them that God our Father is a perfect dad. He drew a comparison between God and an earthy dad. Even the best earthly father is still an imperfect, sinful dad. Yet if a good dad on earth knows how to answer requests from his children and bless them with good gifts, how much more will our perfect heavenly Father do the same? Jesus' point is to encourage us not to have fear but to have faith in praying to our Father.

Jesus' answer to the disciples' request to teach them to pray is about receiving the gift of the Holy Spirit because, while Trinitarian prayer is directed to the Father, it is empowered by the Spirit.

Did you know that the Holy Spirit has been praying throughout eternity? God the Father, God the Son, and God the Spirit have been living in love and communicating that love together forever.

Perhaps the Bible's best-known Trinitarian statement is, "God is love."[c] Or, to say it another way, the triune God is like a perfect relational family and the model for all families.

Love is spoken of roughly eight hundred times throughout Scripture. In stating that "God is love," the Bible reveals the Trinitarian God of the Bible as simultaneously the definition, example, and source of true love. To declare that God is love is to confess that God is Trinitarian.

> God the Father, God the Son, and God the Spirit have been living in love and communicating that love together forever.

Loving requires that there be someone to love, and because our God is in relationship as the Father, Son, and Spirit instead

---

c 1 John 4:8

41

of the lonely concept of one divine Being alone forever held by some religions, our God is love, loved, and loving.

Because God is love, it makes sense that God is relational and created us for relationships with Him and one another. "In the beginning was the Word [Jesus], and the Word was with God [Father], and the Word was God."[d] In the original Greek, John is saying that God the Father and God the Son were pro- verbially face-to-face in eternity past. This language speaks of relationship, which compels us to live face-to-face with others in companionship and connection.

This built-in desire is why we are starving for refreshing rela- tionships. We want to love and be loved, we want to trust and be trusted, and we want to speak and be spoken to in return. What we need is a someone. Your relationship with God is supposed to be your priority, your source of healthy living, and your model for all other relationships. Your relational needs are God sized. Even a good friend, spouse, or parent is a bad god. There is no relationship with anyone that can replace your relationship with God. If you follow the deepest longings of your soul, they will lead you back to the God who made you for a relationship with Him.

Thankfully, God the Spirit, who has lived in perfect relation- ship and loving communication with the Father and Son, lives in the believer. He teaches us how to pray to build a loving relationship with God: "Because you are sons, God has sent the Spirit of his Son into our hearts, crying, 'Abba! Father!'"[e]

Upon salvation, the Spirit dwelling in us begins changing our hearts, and our prayers originate with Him. The Spirit of God brings us into conversation with the Trinity.

d John 1:1
e Galatians 4:6

When I (Mark) was a brand-new Christian, I had no idea how to pray conversationally or from the heart. I had no idea what to do or what to say. I'd never done it. I attended my first Bible study, and because I was the new guy, the leader said, "Mark, since you're new here, why don't you pray for us?"

I said, "Um, not really. That's why I'm here! I don't know what number to dial."

I said, "Why don't *you* pray, and I'll watch." So they bowed their heads and closed their eyes, and I kept one eye open and watched. The Spirit used experiences such as that to teach me. The next thing I knew, I was learning to pray. I didn't read a bunch of books on prayer or go to prayer workshops. I just watched people and started praying, and the Spirit began shaping my heart toward prayer and taught me gradually how to pray.

Teaching a child of God to pray is a lot like teaching a child to speak. The more we hear others doing it, the more we learn to do it ourselves. Christian parents can do a great service for their children by speaking and praying over them and in front of them. This way, the child grows up learning both to speak to people and to pray to God.

Jesus Himself prayed by the Spirit. "He rejoiced in the Holy Spirit and said, 'I thank you, Father, Lord of heaven and earth, that you have hidden these things from the wise and understanding and revealed them to little children; yes, Father, for as such was your gracious will. All things have been handed over to me by my Father, and no one knows who the Son is except the Father, or who the Father is except the Son and anyone to whom the Son chooses to reveal him.'"[f]

This beautiful description of worshipful prayer shows us how

---

f Luke 10:21–22

the Spirit empowers us to pray like Jesus. Since the fruit of the Spirit includes joy, when we pray in the Spirit, we can experience the same kind of joy that Jesus did in prayer. If Jesus prayed, we need to pray. If we have the same Holy Spirit that Jesus did, we can pray like Jesus.

PRAYING THROUGH THE SON

As a young child, Ashley came home from school one day and informed me (Mark) that she needed a good attorney. Curious as to what legal trouble my ponytailed princess could have gotten herself into, I inquired why she needed legal representation.

She proceeded to explain that her friend needed an attorney. A single mother had started attending our church, and God saved her and her little girl, who became Ashley's friend. The father was not very involved in the life of his daughter and only occasionally made his child support payments.

For some reason, he decided to declare legal war on the mother and daughter, threatening to sue for custody if he was not allowed to drop all child support payments. The situation equated to a hostage negotiation with a little girl in the middle. The mother and daughter were understandably afraid because they needed the meager child support to make ends meet. They could not afford an attorney but did not want to have the girl go live with her dad.

Grace and I have always taught our kids that we have money set aside for them to give away to people in need in addition to our giving to the local church and other ministries. We wanted our children to grow up looking for ways to love people by encouraging generosity. Ashley rightly assumed that she had access to sufficient funding to pay for an attorney.

That night, we got a call from the mother. Her daughter had been emphatic that Ashley was paying for their legal bills, and so the mother called to clear up what she thought was confusion over the matter. In the end Ashley paid for the attorney, who won the case, so the mother and daughter could stay together with the financial support they were due.

In this example, Ashley served as the intercessor for her friend. She brought the needs of her friend to us so that we could get her the help she needed. The attorney that Ashley paid for served as the advocate for her friend. The advocate stood before the judge and defended the mother and her daughter.

The Bible says that Jesus "always lives to make intercession"[g] and "we have an advocate with the Father, Jesus Christ."[h] Jesus Christ is both our intercessor, who brings our needs before the Father, and our advocate, who defends us before the Father.

Just as Jesus offered Himself as the atoning sacrifice, becoming our substitute and thereby securing our redemption, He continued after His resurrection and exaltation to stand in the gap for us, interceding for us with the Father. Because "there is one God, and there is one mediator between God and men, the man Christ Jesus,"[i] when we pray to the Father, we are praying by and in the power of the Spirit living in us and we are praying through the power of Jesus Christ living for us.

As we seek to pray through the Son, we should seek to pray as the Son prayed. We notice one thing as we look through the Gospels for instances of Jesus praying: He didn't exactly devote a large amount of time to direct instruction on prayer all at once. Rather, we find that Jesus' direction on prayer is

g Hebrews 7:25
h 1 John 2:1
i 1 Timothy 2:5

woven throughout His life and teaching. His prayers and His teachings on prayer are part of the fabric of His day-to-day life and ministry. He would "pray without ceasing."[j]

Praying without ceasing means we don't have to put on our burlap Jedi robe, climb up a high mountain, get in the lotus position, drink decaf oolong tea, and chant a mantra such as "om." To pray like Jesus means to live a prayerful life, where prayer is a constant and recurring discipline in our lives lived through the Spirit. We get out of bed and pray. We eat breakfast and pray. We get in the car and pray. We go to work and pray. We go shopping and pray. We study and pray. We clean out the garage and pray. Every day and in all facets of our day we have the great privilege of talking to our Father.

Praying like Jesus means living a prayerful life, which begs the next question.

How Did Jesus Pray?

When someone is exceptional, we want to know the secret to their success. This truth applies to world-class athletes, politicians who lead their people to peace and prosperity, business leaders who change markets, moms who raise great kids, and husbands who love their wives well.

The most impactful person in world history is Jesus Christ. In the late nineties, as we approached the new millennium, a *Newsweek* cover story said, "By any secular standard, Jesus is...the dominant figure of Western culture. Like the millennium itself, much of what we now think of as Western ideas, inventions, and values finds its source or inspiration in the religion that worships God in His name. Art and science, the self and society, politics and economics, marriage and the family,

---

j 1 Thessalonians 5:17

right and wrong, body and soul—all have been touched and often radically transformed by Christian influence."[1]

If you aim to learn about basketball, study Michael Jordan. If you desire to learn about political leadership, study Winston Churchill. If you want to learn about prayer, study Jesus Christ.

Now that we've examined Jesus' prayers and Jesus' teaching on prayer for the essential qualities and content of our prayers, it should be helpful to look at a few more of Jesus' prayers. What did Jesus' prayers look like? What kind of prayers did He pray?

Jesus prayed scriptural prayers.

Counselors constantly tell us that a key to any good relationship is communication. A healthy, loving, growing relationship requires that both people speak openly and respectfully and listen carefully and compassionately. What is true of our human relationships is also true of our relationship with God. God speaks to us most clearly through His Word, and we talk to Him in prayer. Because of this, Jesus often prayed Scripture and teaches us to do the same.

Here is one stunning example: "And at the ninth hour Jesus cried with a loud voice, 'Eloi, Eloi, lema sabachthani?'" This lament is a direct quote from Psalm 22:1 and means "My God, my God, why have you forsaken me?"[k]

Jesus was literally praying the Bible, which is how prayer and Bible study go together. The Holy Spirit inspired the writing of Scripture; He indwells us to teach us the Scripture and how to pray according to the Scripture. In prayer, we speak to God, and in Scripture, God speaks to us.

---

k Mark 15:34; Psalm 22:1

If your Bible reading is not going well, pray. If you're confused or feel out of your depth, pray.

Pray before you start reading the Bible. Pray as you're reading, thanking God for His Word and asking God to illuminate its meaning more brightly to you. Pray when you're done reading Scripture and ask God to help you apply what you've read to your daily life.

Read and pray; read and pray; read and pray. Come in prayer to Scripture. When you read something convicting, stop and pray in repentance. When something impresses you, stop and praise God. When something reminds you of someone else, stop and pray for them.

The goal of Bible reading is not for you to get through Scripture but for Scripture to get through you. You might not get through passages quickly, but those passages will stick with you. And you'll enjoy your study time more because it will be shaping you in ways you can't imagine.

If your prayer life is guided by Scripture, then you'll know you are praying in God's will.

I (Ashley) enjoy making to-do lists and checking things off, so for many years I enjoyed intense, long Bible-reading plans that would take me through the Bible in a year or less. I liked being able to tell others how quickly I was reading, but I missed the point of the Bible, which is not about me. I built the habit of reading, which was good, but I didn't let it sink in through prayer and meditation.

> The goal of Bible reading is not for you to get through Scripture but for Scripture to get through you.

More recently, when I read my Bible, I choose a book to go

through at my own pace. I'll read a chapter or two and just wait until a verse or section stands out. Then I'll read it over and over and ask God to show me why He highlighted it. Sometimes God gives me an image to paint in my Bible, sometimes He asks me to memorize it, sometimes He reminds me of a friend to pray for or share it with, and sometimes He connects it to something going on in my life and leads me to pray or journal.

Some days I will meditate on the first verse I read, and sometimes I don't sense anything specific to focus on at first. I try to be patient and ask God to show me one thing to take away from my time with Him, and I find that the more I am in the habit of using my Bible as a communicative tool, the more clearly and quickly I can hear.

Jesus prayed long prayers.

Some of my earliest memories of prayer are around the dinner table or before bedtime. God certainly welcomes these short prayers, but just as when you're getting to know a friend, sometimes you need to sit for a few hours and exchange stories and testimonies.

When I got involved with the prayer tent in college, we would sign up for one-hour blocks to pray, worship, read the Bible, and just be with God. Since I didn't have classes on Fridays, I signed up for a three-hour block in the afternoons.

I remember going to the tent my first week and wondering what I would do sitting there for three hours alone, trying to focus on God. In the end I had this shift for a year and a half, and wow, did God do some cool things within that three-hour time frame.

I shared the gospel with people that God seemingly escorted into the tent to meet me, cried and repented of my sin on countless occasions, prayed for friends and family, and felt God's heart for my very lost college campus.

Some weeks the time would zoom by, but some weeks I had a hard time keeping my mind from distraction and boredom. Some weeks I felt as if I didn't have time for my shift or just wasn't in the mood, but if I hadn't learned to pray lengthy prayers, I know I would have missed out on many opportunities to see God move in my life and the lives of others.

Jesus didn't necessarily pray long prayers publicly, but He spent lengthy amounts of time in prayer with the Father: "In these days he went out to the mountain to pray, and all night he continued in prayer to God."[1] Praying is one way of battling in the unseen realm, which explains why Jesus prayed all night before picking the twelve. We can only imagine the nightlong wrestling in prayer that took place about choosing Judas.

Many (perhaps most) times, you should pray succinctly, but there are times when the best thing we can do is get alone and fight the long battles on our knees until we surrender to the will of God. Whether you're facing a crisis or the imminence of a major life decision, we encourage you to get lots of time alone in prayer.

Before I (Mark) married Grace, I prayed a lot. She did the same. We also asked our Christian friends and family to join us. Since we were young, we did not want simply to ask God to bless our plan, but we wanted to ask God to give us His plan. Are you getting married? Sort that out with God first. Whom you marry is the second-most important decision you will ever make after whom you will worship. The same is true of any major life decision. One of our pastors, who has taught us a lot, walked with us through the biggest decision-making

---

1 Luke 6:12

season of our life as a married couple. We took months to pray and asked others to pray with us and for us. We wanted God to tell us whether we should stay in a ministry, home, and city that we had been serving for a few decades or if we should transition into a completely unknown future in faith.

After months of prayer God spoke to us both audibly at the same time. Grace was in the kitchen, and I was in the bedroom on the opposite end of our home. Grace came running in the bedroom to tell me that God had spoken to her, and stunned, I told her that at the same moment He spoke to her, he also spoke to me. He told us both we were "released."

This word from the Lord led to the biggest faith step of our lives, as we did not know what was next but knew that a season of our life had ended and we needed to step out together in faith. In submission to the pastoral authority over us, we asked our overseers whether they agreed this was a word from God. They confirmed what God said.

Without months of praying together and God supernaturally answering this prayer, we would have been divided, and, as Jesus taught, our household would have fallen apart. Thankfully because of prayer, we were united and able to lead our five kids through an incredibly painful and difficult time. We are now in the holiest, happiest, and healthiest season of our lives, doing ministry together because God heard and answered our prayers.

Jesus prayed warfare prayers.

In any battle a soldier must know how to handle their weapon properly. If not, they will be defeated and destroyed. The famous section of Scripture on spiritual warfare against the devil and demons ends by urging us to pray "at all times in the Spirit, with all prayer and supplication. To that end, keep alert with all perseverance, making supplication for all the saints."[m]

Prayer is war. We learn this principle from Jesus. He spent forty days in prayer, and the devil showed up to attack Him. Do not be surprised when life gets more difficult at the same time your prayer life gets more devoted.

How should we pray when we're betrayed or hurt or confused or in great pain?

Take a look at Jesus' prayer:

"Now is my soul troubled. And what shall I say? 'Father, save me from this hour'? But for this purpose I have come to this hour. Father, glorify your name." Then a voice came from heaven: "I have glorified it, and I will glorify it again."[n]

When Jesus faced the cross, He took His pain to God in prayer. The more we are hurting, the more we need to be praying—not to dishonor God, curse God, blame God, or disobey God, but to present our pain to God as Jesus did.

> Do not be surprised when life gets more difficult at the same time your prayer life gets more devoted.

You can be honest with God. He's God; He can take it. Tell Him how you feel. "God, I'm troubled. I'm struggling right now. I'm hurting very badly." It's OK to say those things to God. Jesus did.

Through prayer Jesus saw there was purpose in His pain. With the cross on the horizon, Jesus did not call out, "Get Me out of this!" He called out, "Get Me through this."

---

m Ephesians 6:10–20 (quote is verse 18)
n John 12:27–28

Jesus prayed that He'd be betrayed *well*, that He'd be abandoned *well*, that He would suffer *well*, and that He would die *well*. It is not always God's will to take our pain away, but it is always God's will to conform us to the image of His Son through our pain.

If you are hurting, suffering, or dying right now, make it your prayer to learn how to hurt, suffer, and die to the glory of God. Such prayers will increase your love for Jesus and appreciation for the pain He suffered in your place. And such prayers will help you respond to God and others with love and grace, as Jesus did amid the pain of His crucifixion.

> It is not always God's will to take our pain away, but it is always God's will to conform us to the image of His Son through our pain.

Pray that God would keep you faithful as you walk through your valley of the shadow of death. God was glorified even in Christ's sufferings, and He will be glorified in yours if you will pray to Him to get you through it. Sometimes prayer gets us around our troubles. Most of the time, prayer gets us through them.

Jesus prayed thankful prayers.

In high school I (Ashley) went through a period of being frustrated that many of my plans weren't working out, and I started to lose sight of what God was doing in the midst of it all. My mom lovingly challenged me to think back and remember all the ways God had blessed me in the past so that I could trust Him to do so again in the future. I started to write down God's blessings on note cards. I had a note card for each day of the year, and for about two and a half years, I wrote one thing that I was thankful for each night before going to bed.

I noticed my mindset slowly started to change as I became grateful instead of grouchy. Although I eventually stopped this specific practice, I go back to journaling a list of things I'm thankful for anytime I feel myself slip back into ungratefulness. I usually end up crying when I realize all that God has blessed me with, even though many of them are simple things that I take for granted.

> Sometimes prayer gets us around our troubles. Most of the time, prayer gets us through them.

Perhaps the most common prayer Jesus prayed was a prayer of thanks. If you are interested in learning how to pray like Jesus, I (Mark) can think of no better prayer habit for you to begin with than to "give thanks in all circumstances."[o]

Here is one example from Jesus' prayer life:

> At that time Jesus declared, "I thank you, Father, Lord of heaven and earth, that you have hidden these things from the wise and understanding and revealed them to little children; yes, Father, for such was your gracious will."[p]

In this instance Jesus is succinctly yet deeply thanking the Father for His gracious revelation of Himself to us. It is a worshipful prayer, a theological prayer, and an insightful prayer. But it is first and foremost a thankful prayer.

Do you want to begin building momentum in your prayer life? Perhaps you ought to start by asking yourself, "What should I thank God for?" The answers to that question are endless, so get started and don't stop. As you do that, it builds

---

o 1 Thessalonians 5:18
p Matthew 11:25–26

hope, anticipation, and expectation inside you. It will make you a God seeker and a grace giver. And it will make prayer abound in your life.

When I (Ashley) was little, the prayers we prayed most often were "thankful prayers." We sought to celebrate God's presence and provision in our lives and the lives of others. To this day the majority of our family dinners together contain this same habit that feeds the soul as the food nourishes our body.

Jesus prayed in song.

The timing of Jesus' death was the Jewish celebration of Passover. It was customary for those partaking in the Passover meal to conclude by singing Psalm 113–118 as a prayer. This practice had been passed down among God's people from generation to generation.

Mark 14:26 says that Jesus and His disciples "had sung a hymn." A Bible commentator familiar with the Jewish custom explains: "It was customary to sing the Hallel antiphonally, one member of the table company chanting the text, and the others responding to each half verse with the shout of praise, 'Hallelujah.' Jesus took the words of these psalms as his own prayer of thanksgiving and praise. He pledged to keep his vows in the presence of all the people (Ps. 116:12–19); he called on the Gentiles to join in the praise of God (Ps. 117); and he concluded with a song of jubilation reflecting his steadfast confidence in his ultimate triumph: 'I shall not die, but live, and declare the works of the Lord' (Ps. 118:17). In the assurance that the rejected stone had been made the keystone by God's action Jesus found a prophecy of his own death and exaltation…When Jesus arose to go to Gethsemane, Ps. 118 was on his lips. It provided an appropriate description of how God would guide his Messiah through distress and suffering to glory."[2]

To prepare His followers for His death, Jesus led them in song as His way of praying as a group. Often we think of singing to God as worship, which it is. But singing to God is also prayer, as it takes the longings of our hearts and verbalizes them with the words in our voices. The church father Augustine said, "With Psalms and hymns you pray to God."[3]

Indeed, we pray individually, as Jesus did. And we pray in a group, as Jesus did, including singing songs as a form of prayer with the rest of God's people in worship.

Jesus used His last breath to pray.

One of the great honors of ministry is being invited into the most sacred moments of people's lives. A pastor gets to visit a newborn baby and mother in the hospital, baptize a new believer, officiate the wedding of a loving couple, and sit at the deathbed of a person as they take their final breaths. Who people surround themselves with, what they do, and what they say in the last hours of their lives reveals a lot about who they are at the deepest level.

In the Gospel of Mark we are given a summary of Jesus' final hours before dying on the cross. Jesus spent the entire night in prayer all alone, as His disciples failed to join Him in prayer. Jesus was "greatly distressed and troubled," saying, "My soul is very sorrowful, even to death." Seeking to process His coming pain, Jesus kept praying the same thing repeatedly: "Again he went away and prayed, saying the same words."[q]

Jesus was not only failed by His friends but also betrayed by His pretend friend, Judas Iscariot. Hanging on the cross, dying

---

q Mark 14:32–42 (Verses 33–34 and 39 are quoted.)

for our sins, enduring the wrath of God, Jesus then said His final words, which were a prayer. "Then Jesus, calling out with a loud voice, said, 'Father, into your hands I commit my spirit!' And having said this he breathed his last."[r]

Before He died, the very last thing Jesus did was pray. The person who prays every day is always ready for their final day. Not only does prayer get us through this life, but it also gets us into the next life, where we see all our prayers answered forever.

REFLECTION

1. Do you have any fears or shame about prayer that you can confess to the Father? If so, what are they?

2. Describe your favorite way to pray (for example, silently, out loud, alone, in a group, journaling, singing).

3. Think about a good father you know and how they interact and converse with their child. What can you learn from them about talking with your Father through prayer?

4. Spend some time in prayer today, and before you do, invite the Holy Spirit to help you learn how to pray to God as Father from your heart. As you pray, thank Jesus that He intercedes for you and brings your prayers to the Father.

5. What thing do you struggle to trust God with in your life? Spend some time today discussing that

---

r Luke 23:46

with the Lord, as well as discussing your fears
about it with Him.

6. Do you usually rush through prayer or set aside
specific time for it? If you need to set aside specific
time, list it here.

7. Describe any big decisions or burdens that you can
talk about with the Father.

Chapter 4

JESUS' WHO, WHAT, HOW, WHEN, AND WHERE OF PRAYER

*And rising very early in the morning, while it was still dark, he
departed and went out to a desolate place, and there he prayed.*
—MARK 1:35

A s I (ASHLEY) took teaching classes in college, I was
encouraged to reflect on how I learned language as
a child: the strategies, methods, and approaches that
worked for me. I realized that I have many vivid memories
of having fun with a song, game, or competitive activity in
Spanish class but few memories of memorizing vocabulary
lists or completing worksheets. However, I know this is how
most of my time was spent.

If you enjoy something, you'll probably learn it faster, and
it will stick because you'll be motivated to keep practicing
and improving. When teaching English to adult immigrants, I
prefer to focus on communication, conversation, and interaction. I get to know the students and their interests and needs
so that I can create learning material that teaches them what
they need to know in a relatable way that reflects how they
communicate in the real world.

Jesus' teaching on prayer uses a similar method from which

we can all benefit. He was constantly in prayer, so He both modeled it to His disciples and taught explicitly about it. But you won't find a book of the Bible named How to Pray. Jesus' teaching on prayer was responsive to His audience and woven into everything He did and said. He told the Pharisees to stop being showy and religious. He told the disciples to pray to God as Father. They had different struggles that He met with different advice.

Because God has a unique relationship with each of His children, He highlights different methods and practices of prayer for each one of us. Prayer is a conversation that constantly goes back and forth, and we learn new elements as we progress in our walk with Him. In this chapter we highlight some of the practical details of Jesus' prayer life to give an idea of the depth and breadth of His teaching on prayer.

HOW SHOULD WE PRAY?

How should we pray? That little question opens up big blessings.

Pray in faith.

To have any healthy relationship requires trust—or, to use a Bible word, faith. If you do not believe that the other person cares for you, is honest with you, and is loyal to you, there simply cannot be any kind of closeness. This principle is true of both our relationships with other people and our relationship with God. For this reason Jesus says, "And whatever you ask in prayer, you will receive, if you have faith."[a]

Having faith in God—that He exists, loves us, wants to take care of us, hears us, gives us the Spirit to teach us to pray, and wants to provide for us—is to prayer what a hurricane is to a

---

a Matthew 21:22

60

kite. Faith helps us to remember that God is our Dad, and like all parents, He has different ways of answering our requests. Sometimes we pray for things, and we lament, "God didn't answer my prayer." But He did. He just said no. No is an answer.

God the Father has three potential answers to all prayers: yes, no, or later.

I (Mark) remember some years ago when we were on vacation staying in a hotel. It was bedtime, and three of our kids made requests. The first kid came up and said, "Dad, I'm hungry. Can I have some grapes?"

"Yes."

The next one approached and said, "Dad, I'm thirsty. Can I have a soda?"

"No. There's no bedtime soda. You don't have to stay up to study for midterms; you're six. Have some water."

The third one came up and said, "Dad, I liked swimming with you today. Can we go swimming again right now?"

"Later. We'll swim again. But not at ten o'clock at night. Right now it's time for bed."

Three kids, three requests. I don't love any of them any less than the others. All three are my children whom I love and want to please. But based on the nature and timing of their requests, they got three different answers.

And that's how God answers us; based on the nature and timing of our requests, we can either receive a yes, no, or later.

One of the simplest ways to pray in faith is to pray with the belief that God hears our prayers. However, not getting what we want doesn't mean God isn't answering. In addition to the Lord's will, there is also the Lord's timing. Often when we make a request that is not immediately answered, it may be that it is not yet the Lord's timing to answer yes, so the answer is later.

Pray succinctly.

Everyone seems to know "that person"—the one who is determined to be holier than God. They like to do religious things in front of other people, such as praying over a meal. And they pray forever. It's long and drawn out and wordy. They get out a thesaurus and make sure to include random spiritual words such as *hallelujah* and *Shekinah glory* while trying to sound impressive, spiritual, and serious. These folks can pray in King James English until the food is cold and everybody's an atheist.

They seem to think that Jesus is in heaven saying, "Oh, wow, that's a good one. I found the coach for our Olympic prayer team!"

Other folks fire off words like flares, trying to vie for Jesus' attention, as if Jesus were up there distracted or asleep until: "What was that? Oh, I got a 'hallelujah,' and I think I hear yelling and see a praise flag. I better pay attention now."

Jesus says:

> But when you pray, go into your room and shut the door and pray to your Father who is in secret. And your Father who sees in secret will reward you. And when you pray, do not heap up empty phrases as the Gentiles do, for they think that they will be heard for their many words.[b]

You don't get bonus points for long and fancy prayers. On the contrary, Jesus is saying that when you pray for recognition and attention, you aren't focused on the Father but rather yourself.

---

b Matthew 6:6–7

Jesus condemns religious people who pray showy prayers for the approval of others or to get their attention. Jesus says that such people "receive the greater condemnation."[c]

To be sure, it is fine to use prayer as a time to process verbally and heal emotionally with God. The psalms are filled with examples of these kinds of laments. But much of the time, the simple, from-the-heart, to-the-point prayers are best.

One example comes from one of our children who was just two years old at the time. They said, "Jesus, You rock. Amen."

It's OK to pray short prayers. You don't need to drag it out; you don't need to speak the King's English; you don't need to yell, stomp your feet, or run banging on a tambourine; and you don't need to know magical words. Speak from your heart. Be respectful, but you don't need to impress your audience. Just talk to your Father.

Pray in God's will.

Have you ever gone online and ordered something, and then it never got delivered? Prayer can feel like that if we are honest. Sometimes we wonder how to understand "Ask, and you will receive," and we're thinking, "Well, I asked, but I didn't receive. What's going on?"

Usually, this happens for one of two reasons: (1) what we are asking for is not in accordance with God's will, or (2) we personally are not in accordance with God's will.

Jesus says:

> Truly, truly, I say to you, whatever you ask of the Father in my name, he will give it to you. Until now you have asked nothing in my name. Ask, and you will receive, that your joy may be full.[d]

---

c Mark 12:40
d John 16:23–24

Asking in Jesus' name is asking within God's will. To pray in Jesus' name is not just to say His name but to pray in accordance with His will, according to His character.

What is God's will? The best way to find God's will is to read God's Word. God's Word tells you that He wants you to grow, so pray that God will nurture you. God's Word tells you that He wants you to pray for your enemies, so pray for your enemies. God wants you to pray for those in leadership, so pray for leaders. These are all examples of praying according to God's will, because they line up with what He tells us in His Word.

Some of us pray against God's will, which explains why God is not answering. If you are asking that God would help you sin, do something foolish, or bring wrongful harm to another person, then God's answer is no. Anything that falls outside of what God's Word tells us to do is not a prayer in "Jesus' name."

Some of us want God to bless relationships we shouldn't be in, to prosper corrupt or unethical businesses, or to condone things we shouldn't be doing. That's not praying in God's will; that's praying in *our* will and asking God to obey us. Prayer doesn't work that way.

What does it mean to pray to the Father in the name of Jesus? It means we do not ask for things that run contrary to the honor of Jesus or that come from a place of disobedience to Jesus. Before we ask God to bless our will, we ask God what His will is for us. Remember, Jesus taught us to pray, "Your will be done,"[e] and prayed His own prayer of surrender: "Not my will, but yours, be done."[f]

e Matthew 6:10
f Luke 22:42

Pray humbly.

Jesus shares a fascinating parable in Luke 18 about two guys going up to the temple to pray. Think of it as two guys in our day bumping into each other at church. One guy is super religious and very determined to create performance art out of his prayer. We will call him Religious Ricky. He prays proudly and loudly, something akin to "I thank You, God, that I'm not a disgusting loser like all these other guys." And he refers to one of the other guys and says, "I especially thank You that I'm not like this guy." We will call the other guy Larry the Loser.

Upon hearing the prayer of Religious Ricky, Larry the Loser had to be thinking, "Hey, wait a minute."

Religious Ricky's entire prayer is about how awesome he thinks he is, how much better he is than everybody else, and thanking God for making him so awesome. If you read his prayer, it's a parade of I, I, I, and me, me, me.

Larry the Loser's prayer consists simply and succinctly and humbly of this: "God, be merciful to me, a sinner!" He is honest about his state before God. He's not seeking people's approval; he's seeking God's help. The difference is not that Ricky and Larry are sinners; the difference is that only Larry knows it.

Jesus said, "I tell you, this man went down to his house justified, rather than the other. For everyone who exalts himself will be humbled, but the one who humbles himself will be exalted."g

Larry didn't pray long. But he prayed respectfully and humbly, and God honored his prayer.

The truth is, we each have a bit of Religious Ricky in us. "Lord, help this person learn as much as I have." "Lord, make this person see things the way I do." "Lord, help this person

---

g Luke 18:14

become like me." "Lord, teach this person to do what I want." "Lord, help this person appreciate all I have done for them." "Lord, convict this person so they feel awful for what they did and apologize to me." "Lord, please punish this person for what they did to me."

Those are awful, arrogant prayers.

God honors a humble heart, so pray humbly with the acknowledgment that you are a sinner saved by grace, that God is in control and you are not, and that no amount of self-righteousness or prayerful performance will ever beat God in a spiritual arm wrestling match.

The point of the parable is this—if you humbly look up to God, you won't arrogantly look down on others. In this way, how we pray tells us a lot about where we are looking.

Pray fervently.

One thing you learn about prayer from kids is how resilient they can be when they want something. When a child makes a request that is not quickly granted for any reason, the child often keeps making the request over and over and over.

If we are to pray for something in God's will, then it's a good thing to keep praying. Keep praying! Don't just pray once and move on. Keep at it. Cultivate it as a discipline in your life. "[Jesus] told them a parable to the effect that they ought always to pray and not lose heart."[h]

Have you been praying for something for a long time that you know is in God's will? Keep praying. Why? First, because you'll keep hoping. Fervent prayer keeps your heart inclined toward God and His blessings because love "always hopes."[i]

Second, fervent prayer will maintain a willingness in you to

---

h Luke 18:1
i 1 Corinthians 13:7, NIV

66

grow and be changed. If you stop praying for people, you will stop caring about them. But if you keep praying for them, your heart will grow more tender toward them.

For example, if you're single and feeling called to marriage, keep praying for your future spouse. Not only is doing this a great gift to your future spouse, but it also helps guard your own heart against temptation while you wait.

If you keep praying for people, you will grow in love for people. If you keep praying for God's help and blessings in your life, you will grow in love for God.

Wait and pray in hope, and this hopeful, fervent expectancy will conform your heart to the will of God. In this way, fervent prayer prepares us for God to answer our prayer.

WHAT (AND WHOM) SHOULD WE PRAY FOR?

Having studied some qualities and characteristics of Trinitarian prayer, we will now consider the content. What and whom should we pray for?

Pray for sinners.

If asking God to bless you is the equivalent of swimming in the shallow end of the prayer pool, then asking God to bless your enemies is swimming in the deep end. Jesus said, "Whenever you stand praying, forgive, if you have anything against anyone, so that your Father also who is in heaven may forgive you your trespasses."[j]

"But what if they don't apologize?" you might ask.

Forgive them.

"What if they never change and don't think they did anything wrong?"

---

j Mark 11:25

Forgive them.

Praying this way doesn't mean you ignore reality and pretend everything's fine. It doesn't mean you trust that person or will be close to them. But it does mean you give up the inclination to seek vengeance, which is natural, and you replace it with forgiveness, which is supernatural.

As David did, ask God to search the depths of your heart so that your sin may be exposed, softening your heart toward others as you experience God's forgiving heart toward you.[k]

Praying for someone means you love them, so praying for those who have sinned against you is a way of obeying the Lord's command to love your enemies. And when you pray for someone, it begins the healing process so that you can move on from the person who hurt you to the person who can heal you.

Pray for your needs.

Some people are self-reliant and don't like to ask for help. Knowing we all need help, Jesus taught, "Ask, and it will be given to you; seek, and you will find; knock, and it will be opened to you. For everyone who asks receives, and the one who seeks finds, and to the one who knocks it will be opened."[1]

> When you pray for someone, it begins the healing process so that you can move on from the person who hurt you to the person who can heal you.

What Jesus is saying is: *ask*. Don't get super spiritual and self-conscious, thinking God will get frustrated with you any more than a kid who is asking their loving dad

---

k Psalm 139:23
l Matthew 7:7–8

for something to eat or help with a task. If you have a need, bring it to your Father. He loves you.

Like any good parent, the Father is committed to practical provisions. Any good mom will tell you that getting snacks and drinks for the child that asks is not a burden but a blessing and a way to show their love to their child.

Please don't think your concerns are too little for God. You are God's child, which means you are His blessing and not a burden.

Some years ago while I was working on a book project with a tight deadline, Ashley came up asking for my help with her Dora the Explorer sticker book. As a little girl, she loved learning Spanish and doing stickers—so this was a double dose of delight. Her fingers were too little, but my big, furry fingers seem naturally designed to peel off Dora stickers. Now, my daughter was not thinking, "Oh, Dad is under a book deadline; I better not bother him. He's too important and busy." She was thinking, "My Daddy loves me and likes to help me."

I love my daughter and want to be involved in *all* of her life. If her urgent problem was removing Dora stickers, then it needed to move to the top of my priority list. Why? Because she was at the top of my priority list. Praying for our needs is, for God, not as much about the needs as the relationship. God made us dependent beings with needs, and when we invite Him to meet those needs, it builds our relationship.

Your Father wants to help you! And the good news is that He never gets overwhelmed because He has no limitations. Even the best parent can get worn out by their kids, but not God the Father.

If something is a concern to you, big or small, bring it to

God in prayer. You'll never know whether He'll say yes if you don't ask.

Do you need a job? Ask. Do you need a spouse? Ask. Do you need to grow? Ask. Do you need help? Ask. Do you need healing? Ask. Do you need a burden lifted? Ask. Do you need a question answered? Ask. Do you need a break? Ask.

Pray for your burdens.

In one of the most difficult seasons of our lives, Grace and I met weekly with a Christian pastor and licensed counselor. He is a godly, older man that we love as a spiritual father. Each time we met, we brought him our burdens, as we were under the highest levels of stress and anxiety that we had ever experienced. Every time, he took us and our burdens to prayer. Sometimes our hour-long meetings were five minutes of talking and fifty-five minutes of praying.

As he prayed, he would sometimes walk over to us and make a motion as if he were lifting some weight off us, carrying it over to the garbage can, and spiritually dumping it. This practice went on for months, and bit by bit through prayer, he helped us take our burdens off and hand them to Jesus to carry them for us and with us. Tragically religious people only add burdens to us until they crush us. Jesus warned of these people. "They tie up heavy burdens, hard to bear, and lay them on people's shoulders, but they themselves are not willing to move them with their finger."[m] In contrast, Spirit-filled people "bear one another's burdens."[n]

One ox is a powerful animal. Two oxen pulling together multiply their power. One farming expert says, "While a team of oxen can pull its own body weight at a walking pace, for

---

m Matthew 23:4
n Galatians 6:2

short bursts of six to eight feet, a well-trained team of oxen can pull up to [two to three] times their body weight—or as much as 12,000 to 13,000 pounds."[1]

Jesus uses this very analogy to speak of prayer as yoking together with Him to pull whatever burden is on us: "Come to me, all who labor and are heavy laden, and I will give you rest. Take my yoke upon you, and learn from me, for I am gentle and lowly in heart, and you will find rest for your souls. For my yoke is easy, and my burden is light."[o]

In prayer, we transfer much of the weighty burden we are carrying to Jesus, who carries it for us and with us. Until the burden is transferred, we're not praying to God as much as we are complaining to God.

Pray against temptation.

The adage "The best defense is a good offense" has been applied to everything from board games to sports and military combat. The same is true of our spiritual life.

Too often we sin and pray our repentant apologies after we sin (which we *should* do!); too seldom do we pray preemptively, guarding our hearts against sin before it's too late. Jesus says, "Watch and pray that you may not enter into temptation. The spirit indeed is willing, but the flesh is weak."[p]

We all have weak spots, places in our lives where we drift away from God's will. We all have different appetites—sex, food, alcohol, money, anger, work, and so on. We should be praying that God would strengthen us in those areas, help us satisfy those appetites in godly ways, and steer us away from people, places, and thoughts that tempt us to indulge them in sinful ways.

o Matthew 11:28–30
p Matthew 26:41

Pray in advance against temptation. Make up your mind ahead of time to agree with God on where you are weak to wander into sin.

Some prayers throughout the Book of Psalms strike a more military tone. In those prayers, people are praying against an enemy, praying against temptation, confessing their weakness and vulnerability, and crying out to God from the midst of a battle for strength and deliverance. These kinds of prayers against our enemy and his temptations are similar to weary soldiers under heavy enemy fire calling to a general for backup and support before they are overtaken. Praying against temptation is like that.

Pray for evangelists and church planters.

As I was preaching a series that covered the entire Book of Daniel, our church family was stunned by an amazing story. At the time of Daniel, the people of God had been away from their home in Israel for seventy years. As a result, the temple (their church) had been closed, and there needed to be evangelists and church planters to travel back to Israel to replant the temple and bring the gospel of Jesus Christ to the nations.

At the beginning of Daniel 10 he prayed that God would open an opportunity for this exact ministry. Daniel 10:10–13 reports:

> And behold, a hand touched me and set me trembling on my hands and knees. And he said to me, "O Daniel, man greatly loved, understand the words that I speak to you, and stand upright, for now I have been sent to you." And when he had spoken this word to me, I stood up trembling. Then he said to me, "Fear not, Daniel, for from the first day that you set your heart to understand and humbled yourself before your God, your words have been heard, and I have

come because of your words. The prince of the kingdom of
Persia withstood me twenty-one days, but Michael, one of
the chief princes, came to help me."

Daniel prayed for what we would call evangelism and
church planting. Three weeks later, a divine being arrived to
tell him that his prayer was immediately answered, but that
the visit from the divine being to answer the prayer resulted
in twenty-one days of spiritual warfare with a demonic entity
called the Prince of Persia. The divine being was losing the
spiritual battle until Michael, one of the most powerful angels
in the Bible, showed up to help them win the war. The point is
that we need to be praying for evangelists and church planters
because tremendous spiritual warfare occurs in the unseen
realm when attempts are made to expand the kingdom of God.

Jesus says, "The harvest is plentiful, but the laborers are few;
therefore pray earnestly to the Lord of the harvest to send out
laborers into his harvest."q Pray for those who love Jesus, love
people, and love to bring the message of Jesus to people. The
gift of evangelism is a special thing, a powerful thing. If you
are serious about the Great Commission, you must pray not
only for your opportunities to share the gospel but also for the
evangelists, church planters, and apostolic church leaders so
that the kingdom of God continues to conquer the darkness of
this wicked world.

The world needs more churches, not fewer. The world needs
more godly leaders, not fewer. The world needs more evangelists, not fewer. Praying in this manner opens your heart and
eyes to do more evangelism in your own life by sharing Jesus
with those you come in contact with and opening your wallet
to support the cause of Team Jesus.

---

q Matthew 9:37–38

Pray for your enemies.

In the Book of Acts, an early church leader named Stephen is murdered by a mob of angry religious men led by the religious terrorist Saul of Tarsus. While dying, Stephen echoed Jesus and prayed for his murderers, "Lord, do not hold this sin against them."[r] Stephen then died, seeing Jesus get off His throne in heaven to cheer like a fan at the best part of a sporting event. Within a few pages, Jesus answered Stephen's prayer by saving Saul, changing his name to Paul, and sending him out to write roughly half the books of the New Testament, which include repeated, detailed gospel truth about forgiveness. When we, like Stephen, follow Jesus' example of praying for our enemies, amazing things often happen.

To forgive our enemies is to obey Jesus. "I say to you, Love your enemies and pray for those who persecute you."[s] On the cross, where those who hated Him had hung Him to die, Jesus prayed for forgiveness for His enemies: "Father, forgive them, for they know not what they do."[t] Included in Jesus' prayer were you and I. Through sin, we are Jesus' enemies, but He prayed for us and then died to answer His own prayer so that we could be forgiven.

Praying for your enemies also keeps you from becoming like them. The natural response to being hurt is hate. But once we have welcomed bitterness and hate into our hearts, we have poisoned our souls. The supernatural response to evil is self-control, responding to God rather than our enemies, and treating them as God treated us when we were His enemies. Praying for our enemies is a gift that we give to them and ourselves.

---

r Acts 7:60
s Matthew 5:44
t Luke 23:34

Pray for your friends.

One of Jesus' nearest and dearest friends was Peter, whom He prayed for: "Simon, Simon, behold, Satan demanded to have you, that he might sift you like wheat, but I have prayed for you that your faith may not fail. And when you have turned again, strengthen your brothers."[u]

If you love your friends, pray for your friends. Pray for them all the things you pray for yourself: mercy, wisdom, strength, health, provision.

And don't just *tell* them you'll pray for them. *Do it.*

If a friend asks you to pray for them, stop right there, put a hand on them, and pray for them. Connect with them and love on them.

Pray for friends while on the phone with them. Pray for them when you get an email or text from them. Pray for them when you see them, and pray for them when you don't. Tell them that you've prayed for them. Hearing this will greatly encourage them.

Prayer also works as pre-evangelism for friends you don't even have yet!

Going into college at a huge state university, I (Ashley) didn't know a single person. In my dorm on move-in day, I started to pray that God would bring me Christian friends. I was invited to a church the next day and immediately knew it was where God wanted me to start meeting the friends I had been praying to find. I felt so at home and at peace.

Usually non-Christians we pray for are grateful, and even if they're not followers of Jesus, they're willing to appreciate prayers made for them. So pray for your friends. And pray

---

u Luke 22:31–32

for people who are not yet your friends—many of them will become your friends because you prayed for them.

Pray for children.

Grace and I (Mark) started praying over Ashley and her siblings shortly after they were conceived by laying hands on Grace's tummy. When each of our kids was born, the first thing we did was hold them and pray over them. Every night at bedtime, we laid hands on them and prayed over them. Every child should be prayed for as Jesus modeled. "Children were brought to him that he might lay his hands on them and pray."[v]

Pray for your kids. Pray for other people's kids. Pray for kids in your family, kids in your church, and kids in your neighborhood. You don't even have to have kids to pray for kids. Jesus was single, and He prayed for the children.

When you pray for children, children will learn how to pray.

When one of Ashley's brothers was about eighteen months old, he was already putting his hands together at bedtime and praying. He only knew about four words, but he was talking to Jesus. It was awesome. He learned to do that by seeing his mom and dad and his brothers and sisters and grandparents praying around him and for him.

Another example is a time I will never forget, one night when I heard our then two-year-old son crying in his bedroom. When I went to find out what was wrong, I discovered his four-year-old sister laying hands on her little brother, and she prayed, "Dear Jesus, please help Pooka not be so sad. Amen."

It was beautiful!

She had had other people pray for her when she was sick or

v Matthew 19:13

hurt, and through those experiences, she learned how to pray for her brother.

Pray for your kids and with your kids!

As a kid, I (Ashley) always felt confident that my parents could fix any problem or issue we faced because I would see them pray about it and hear from God. I learned not to fear, because they were so good at praying before panicking or trying to fix it on their own, and they often prayed thankful prayers to remind us of God's faithfulness. It built my faith to trust my parents' wisdom. They taught me to hear from God for myself instead of always acting as a mediator for me, calling many family meetings to pray about ministry opportunities or to pray for one another. I learned that it was normal and important to pray simple prayers of faith because I saw my parents doing it all the time.

When Should We Pray?

Imagine a marriage relationship or a parent-child relationship where they only communicated for a few minutes on Sunday mornings. How shallow would those relationships be?

A prayerful life encompasses all our experiences—life with its highs and lows and all its major and minor details—as we "pray without ceasing."ᵂ

Praying like Jesus means praying for just about everything: all needs, all situations, all people. If you want to pray like Jesus, it means you must also pray without ceasing. For disciples of Jesus, anytime is prayer time. This leads to our next point.

---

w 1 Thessalonians 5:17

Pray daily.

Jesus prayed every day.

The Jews prayed this prayer daily: "Hear, O Israel: the LORD our God, the LORD is one."[x] As a devout Jew, Jesus would have done the same. Because of this, He could quote it freely from memory.[y] Praying was as constant for Jesus as breathing is for us. Not a day went by that Jesus didn't pray.

Pray early.

Praying early in the morning is tough for the night owls. It is not only something Jesus did, but it is also something we should do. "And rising very early in the morning, while it was still dark, he departed and went out to a desolate place, and there he prayed."[z]

For disciples of Jesus, anytime is prayer time.

While it was still dark—that's *early.*

Dedicate your day to the will of God before the phone rings, before the inbox fills up, before the day gets hectic and busy— or, as I (Mark) like to put it, before the false trinity of hurry, worry, and busy steamroll your soul.

Pray at mealtime.

All our problems started with our first parents not praying before they dined with the devil, so we should carefully and prayerfully invite the Lord to our table for every meal. Mealtime prayers seem to be going out of fashion, but even a quick survey of the Gospels shows Jesus praying over meals.

Jesus not only prayed that God would provide daily bread, but He also thanked God for the provision before He ate it as

---

x Deuteronomy 6:4
y Mark 12:29–30
z Mark 1:35

an example for others. "Taking the five loaves and the two fish, he looked up to heaven and said a blessing. Then he broke the loaves and gave them to the disciples, and the disciples gave them to the crowds."aa

Jesus also blessed special meals. "And he took a cup, and when he had given thanks he gave it to them, and they all drank of it."ab And in that same Passover meal that we call the Last Supper, "he took bread, and when he had given thanks, he broke it and gave it to them, saying, 'This is my body, which is given for you. Do this in remembrance of me.'"ac

As Americans we live in a culture of abundance, where obesity is more common than starvation. Even if you do not have much money, chances are you don't go a day without food to eat and water to drink. When was the last time you thanked God for that "ordinary" provision? Millions in the world do not know whether they will eat today. Just because God has been gracious does not mean we should not be grateful.

Thanking God at mealtime shouldn't be shallow or superficial. Don't pray the same thing every time! Pray from your heart. Thank God for the food and the people who prepared it. Then thank God for the people who are joining you for the meal. In some cultures, Christians pray at the end of the meal, thanking God especially for the parts they liked the best. That works too.

WHERE SHOULD WE PRAY?

Praying like Jesus means we should pray where Jesus prayed. And Jesus prayed anywhere and everywhere.

---

aa Matthew 14:19
ab Mark 14:23
ac Luke 22:19

Pray publicly.

Jesus prayed in large groups on many different occasions. His public prayers were nearly always *for* the people present.

> Just because God has been gracious does not mean we should not be grateful.

"When all the people were baptized, and when Jesus also had been baptized and was praying, the heavens were opened."[ad] Jesus raised Lazarus in front of a gawking crowd and then prayed specifically for them. "Jesus lifted up his eyes and said, 'Father, I thank you that you have heard me. I knew that you always hear me, but I said this on account of the people standing around, that they may believe that you sent me.'"[ae] Jesus was not too shy to pray in public. The most frequently mentioned emotion of Jesus in the Bible is compassion, which is why He prayed for people and let them hear Him.

I (Mark) will never forget the day when I was a little boy and a friend's mom saw that I was struggling with an injury and stopped and prayed over me as I sat in the dugout with my baseball team. That one act of kindness opened my mind to God in a major way and has stuck with me ever since. Prayer might seem like a little thing, but so is a key that unlocks a giant cell door to set someone free.

Pray corporately.

Today God's people gather corporately at the church. In Jesus' day God's people met at the temple. He made it clear that we are to pray with God's people in God's house.

---

ad Luke 3:21
ae John 11:41–42

> He was teaching them and saying to them, "Is it not written, 'My house shall be called a house of prayer for all the nations'?"[af]

Rather than ranting about the church on the internet, we must pray for the church on our knees. If the body of Christ prayed when He went to worship, then the body of Christ called the church should pray when it goes to worship.

I (Ashley) believe God wants His church to be united in worship of Him, and the best way to accomplish that is to pray together. Whether this is in a small group in a home or a large church service, praying for those present or other requests, prayer is a bridge that brings believers together no matter their backgrounds. I've been in church services all over the world where I felt the presence of the Holy Spirit, whether I understood the language being spoken or not. Prayer not only shortens the distance between God and us, but it also reduces the distance between fellow believers and us.

> *Prayer might seem like a little thing, but so is a key that unlocks a giant cell door to set someone free.*

Pray in small groups.

Jesus not only prayed in large groups, but He also prayed in small groups. "Now about eight days after these sayings he took with him Peter and John and James and went up on the mountain to pray."[ag]

There's Jesus' small group! Together they went away to meet with one another and to meet with the Lord.

---

af Mark 11:17
ag Luke 9:28

As you pray with other believers, you learn how to pray and what to pray. Sharing prayer requests and praying for those requests together helps create unity and intimacy in the family of God. For the married, one of the most important decisions you must agree on is who you will each turn to for prayer and wise counsel.

Pray privately.

Like with most relationships, what we do in private determines the quality and health of the relationship. A spouse can post nice things on social media and say nice things when family and friends are present, but the invisible life together at home is the real barometer of that relationship.

Private prayer is very, very important to the Christian life.

Jesus prayed publicly in large and small crowds, but He also prayed privately. After ministering to crowds, "he went up on the mountain to pray."[ah] After standing before crowds, Jesus was kneeling before God as "he was praying alone."[ai] The secret to Jesus' power in public was His persistence in private prayer. "But now even more the report about him went abroad, and great crowds gathered to hear him and to be healed of their infirmities. But he would withdraw to desolate places and pray."[aj]

Thousands were coming out to hear Jesus preach and teach; miracles were happening; healings were taking place; demons were getting defeated. His ministry was powerful and therefore demanding. And Jesus needed to get away for a bit to recharge and refresh.

He needed that. And *you* need that.

ah Mark 6:46
ai Luke 9:18
aj Luke 5:15–16

82

While there are many benefits of technology (including e-books and podcasts on prayer), technology can also be a great distraction. Rather than taking things to the Lord, we take things to others. Or we become so distracted by our technology that we do not get much time for silence, solitude, meeting with God, praying to God, and listening to God.

I (Mark) am more introverted and recharged by time alone with God. Ashley is too. Ever since she was a little girl, I understood her need for time alone with God for the development of her soul. Both of us enjoy being out in God's creation alone. I like to head out in my SUV and find a quiet spot outside to hike, journal, pray, and meet with the Lord. She loves to sit in beautiful surroundings to pray, read the Bible, journal, and watercolor.

Sometimes it is good to pray alone and aloud. A good walk or hike can be a perfect time to exercise the soul along with the body. If you'd like to practice prayer walking in the city, just turn your phone off but keep your hands-free kit on. People will just think you're talking to somebody on the phone. After all, it is kind of an international call to heaven.

Or redeem your commute to work. Turn off the technology and speak to God out loud or in silence if you are on the bus. When in a crowd, you can also pray silently by journaling out your prayers to God.

> You cannot give to people in public what you have not gotten from God in private.

In our plugged-in world that is churning away every minute of every day, people are anxious, exhausted, and worn-out. My first car was a 1956 Chevy. One day the ignition got stuck while the engine was running, and I literally could not turn the vehicle off. Unless I unplugged the battery, it would have kept running until it exhausted all its fuel. Many people are like that car. They are stuck with their engines running until they get sick and run out of the physical, emotional, and mental fuel to continue. Private time in prayer with the Lord is how we turn off and get refueled. You cannot give to people in public what you have not gotten from God in private.

REFLECTION

1. Can you think of prayers that God has answered with yes, no, and later? What was your response to each? Looking back, do you understand why He responded the way He did?

2. Is it easier for you to pray for yourself or others? Why? Is there anyone you have a hard time praying for?

3. How much of your prayer life is defensive or reactive, when you pray *after* things have happened to make them stop or to repent? How much of your prayer life is offensive or proactive, when you pray *before* things happen to try to find God's will?

4. What *whos, wheres, whats, whens,* and *hows* of prayer are missing in your life? How can you make them part of your routine?

Chapter 5

THE LORD'S PRAYER

And when you pray, you must not be like the hypocrites. For they love to stand and pray in the synagogues and at the street corners, that they may be seen by others. Truly, I say to you, they have received their reward. But when you pray, go into your room and shut the door and pray to your Father who is in secret. And your Father who sees in secret will reward you. And when you pray, do not heap up empty phrases as the Gentiles do, for they think that they will be heard for their many words. Do not be like them, for your Father knows what you need before you ask him. Pray then like this: Our Father in heaven, hallowed be your name. Your kingdom come, your will be done, on earth as it is in heaven. Give us this day our daily bread, and forgive us our debts, as we also have forgiven our debtors. And lead us not into temptation, but deliver us from evil. For if you forgive others their trespasses, your heavenly Father will also forgive you, but if you do not forgive others their trespasses, neither will your Father forgive your trespasses.
—MATTHEW 6:5–15

O NE OF THE most iconic and beloved photos of all time was taken in the White House. President John F. Kennedy and his wife, Jacqueline, were the first sitting presidential family in nearly eighty years to give birth to a child while in office. John Jr. was in utero during his dad's campaign and grew up in the White House.

The presidential desk his dad worked from was the Resolute desk, which had been a gift from Queen Victoria to Rutherford B. Hayes and has been used by presidents ever since. One day a photographer captured President Kennedy sitting at the desk overseeing the preeminent nation on the planet while his son was playing under the desk and opened what he called the "the secret door" to "my house" and peered out. The now legendary photo showed in one image the simultaneous authority and power of a ruling father and the special loving and intimate relationship his child enjoyed with him that no one else does.

The world's most famous prayer from Jesus Christ is another snapshot of a similar relationship. As the Son of God, Jesus teaches us to pray to God as "Our Father," who rules and reigns over not just a nation but every nation from His throne "in heaven."

THE LORD'S PRAYER

Most of us are at least partly familiar with the Lord's Prayer. You've probably said it at some point in your life at least once, and many of us have it memorized. It's been set to music, recited in worship services, and even plastered on all kinds of products. Its simplicity, coupled with our familiarity with it, has tempted us to forget what great teaching the prayer is for us and just how great a gift it is *to* us.

The Lord's Prayer itself takes up only one short paragraph (just four short lines, depending on the translation). In its context, however, this whole passage constitutes Jesus' message instructing us on how to begin or deepen our parent-child relationship with God.

How *Not* to Pray

In Matthew 6:5–8, Jesus prefaces His teaching on how we should pray by first telling us how we should *not* pray. There are two groups that Jesus highlights as examples of how not to pray: the Pharisees and the Gentiles. In our day, we would consider these groups the religious and the rebellious, respectively.

Jesus was pointedly clear that we should not look to religious people for lessons on prayer. Indeed, while some religions and religious people may seem very pious and serious, Jesus is emphatic that this type of prayer is a problem because it diminishes our relationship with God, which defeats the entire goal of praying. Religious prayer is typically a performance for the approval of a human audience; it is heaping up empty phrases and big words into lengthy prayers, as if God needs to be informed or compelled.

We once had a layover in an airport and got to watch a very overtly religious gentleman in the terminal practicing the art of religious prayer. He had on very clearly religious clothing, complete with a hat big enough to double as the roof of a small home. His choice of hairstyle and beard were overtly intended to tell the world about his religion and that shaving was sinning. He stopped in the middle of the airport and started rocking back and forth, bouncing up and down as if he were experiencing a personal earthquake. All the while, he said his brief prayer mantra over and over again at an incredibly high volume. He made sure to draw the attention of everyone to himself as they were forced to walk around him and, if conversing, talk over him.

This guy was the epitome of "vain repetition." I (Mark) silently stood off to the side and prayed for the guy to meet the real God of the Bible. I was also waiting for him to finish so that I could read him Jesus' words from Matthew 6:5. I got my Bible out and waited a long time. But he just kept on bouncing and rocking and chanting his prayer mantra over and over and over. Eventually I had to catch my flight, but he was still going with no sign of stopping anytime soon.

I'm sure some people would have looked at this guy making a scene in an airport and thought, "Wow, look how serious he is." But Jesus would have us look at this guy and think, "Wow, look how silly he is." Who does he think he's impressing? Certainly not God.

Jesus tells us not to imitate this kind of ridiculous rote religion. We should take God seriously but not ourselves. It's not as if the Father doesn't hear you if you don't face east, wear a special outfit, have a sacred rug to kneel on, or repeat a mantra; you don't need to move a certain way, and you don't have to perform. You *shouldn't* do those things. There might be certain postures or places that help you pray, but just remember that God is not a broken vending machine; you can't rock Him back and forth and pound on Him until some candy falls out.

On the other hand, the Gentiles "heap up empty phrases."[a] These are what I call "dearly belovedisms" or trite, pithy statements that people who don't know God echo from other people who don't know God. Examples include, "When God closes a door, He opens a window," from the book of 1 Nowhere 2:3, and, "You just need to send out good thoughts so that the universe will bless you," which is a direct quote from 2 Nonsense 6:66. God's not broken. Neither is He stingy. Some people think that they have to pry things out of God's clenched fists. As a dad, if one of my kids came up to me and began incessantly repeating, "Iwantapeanutbuttersandwich,   Iwantapeanutbuttersandwich,

---

a Matthew 6:7

Iwantapeanutbuttersandwich," I would say, "OK, got it. You don't have to arm wrestle me to give you something." You don't have to wear the Father down as if He didn't hear you the first time or just needs some extra convincing, as if prayer were a stick and He were a piñata. God is a good Father who knows what we, the kids He loves, need.

The third option is to be like a child. Christian prayer is to be humble, simple, respectful, sincere, and relational; it includes both speaking to and listening to God. By teaching us the Lord's Prayer, Jesus was not telling us what to say, as if His words were to be repeated over and over like an old record stuck in a groove. Instead, He says, "Pray *like* this." His prayer, then, is a model of prayer that, by the power of the indwelling Holy Spirit, we can learn from as our own prayer life matures.

PRAYER THAT IS *CHRISTIAN*

Many of the technological advances in our day are for the same purpose—to increase our ability to communicate with people we love by hearing their voices and seeing their faces. In years past, when technology only allowed you to hear someone's voice but not see their face, the communication was not as deep or effective.

In God's Word we read of a blessed few people who met with God *face-to-face*, the Bible's language for relational friendship, joy, and love. One day, Paul tells us, all Christians will see Jesus Christ "face to face."[b] In the meantime, the closest we get to that experience is prayer.

D. Martyn Lloyd-Jones once wrote, "Prayer is beyond any question the highest activity of the human soul. Man is at his

---

b 1 Corinthians 13:12

greatest and highest when upon his knees he comes face to face with God."[1]

The prospect of this kind of intimacy can be very intimidating, and rightly so. We are weak, sinful, and on a very steep learning curve when it comes to a relationship with God. But Jesus in His goodness and graciousness gave us a template for how to pray. His disciples wanted to know how to pray, and Jesus responded with what we call today the Lord's Prayer.

For starters, we need to make sure we are praying to the right God in the same way that we make sure our bank deposit was made to the proper account, or we confirm we are calling or texting the right number before we share the intimate details of our life. Christians don't pray like those of other religions, and Christians don't pray *with* those of other religions.

Why?

For the same reason that a child with a loving mother should not jump on any random school bus after class and follow any random kid home and walk in the door to call a woman they never met Mom.

> Christians don't pray like those of other religions, and Christians don't pray *with* those of other religions.

Our God is different. Our God is real. Our God is God. Our God is our Father. The Scriptures tell us that all other gods are demons in disguise, and we all know Christians aren't supposed to pray to demons. Sometimes demons will even answer prayers to keep you praying to them, which is part of the power of their deception.

We should be civil, kind, and gracious to people from other religions with other gods. But we cannot pray together with people of other religions as if we are all praying to the same God because we're not in the same family with the same Father.

Christian prayer is Trinitarian: to the Father, through the Son, by the Spirit. The Holy Spirit in a believer teaches us how to pray since He alone is the mediator between God and us. Our prayers are prayed *through* Jesus Christ, the Son of God, and our prayers are ultimately prayed *to* the Father as Jesus taught. Real prayer isn't just vaguely "spiritual" or "religious"— it is distinctly Christian. And the prayer Jesus gives us in the Lord's Prayer shows us six areas of focus that help us dial in our prayer life more clearly.

"Our Father in Heaven": Adoration

The Lord's Prayer begins with the phrase "Our Father." In these two simple terms are two towering truths. One, to be a Christian is to have God the Father lovingly adopt you to be His beloved child. Two, to be a Christian is to have a new spiritual church family with other brothers and sisters who also call on God together as our Father. As a Christian, you cannot be healthy unless you have a relationship with both God as Father and a church as a family.

Some people have a relationship with God as Father, but they are not connected to brothers and sisters in a church family. Often this is because of church hurt from the past. Just as in a family something so hurtful can be said or done that the relationship becomes distant or nonexistent, so in the church family the same hurt does happen.

Your relationship with God is incredibly important, in the same way that a family with multiple children needs to have every child relationally connected to their parent. But most of what the Bible commands cannot be obeyed in isolation. There are about fifty-six occurrences of the phrase "one another" in the twenty-seven books of the New Testament because Christianity is a team sport where we love and serve one another. All the instructions to encourage one another, love one another, serve one another, forgive one another, and pray for one another require being part of the church family. Christianity, like tennis, doesn't work as a solo sport.

> As a Christian, you cannot be healthy unless you have a relationship with both God as Father and a church as a family.

Some people have a relationship with the church, but they are not connected to God as Father. Every church has people who enjoy the loving relationships and support that they find from God's family, which is wonderful. But unless they come to know God as Father, they remain forever lost and separated from the Father. These folks should be welcomed into and loved by the church family with the goal of seeing them also come to know and love the Father.

To call on God as our Father is to join the entire family of God in prayer, which includes brothers and sisters throughout history as well as the billions scattered across the nations speaking to our Father in a host of earthly languages compelled by the same Holy Spirit today. Praying with and for one another is one of the best ways to build our relationship with God and others.

When God is called Father in the first three Gospels (Matthew, Mark, Luke), the word is always on the lips of Jesus. Again, this is not commonplace in ancient religions but rather a revolutionary understanding of the nature of God that Jesus taught us, starting with His first disciples.

My kids teach me (Mark) a lot about prayer. One night my wife, Grace, and I went out on a date before we had our current total of five kids. After we came home, I snuggled up at bedtime with Alexie, our then four-year-old daughter. We sang some songs (despite my awful singing voice), read some Bible stories, and said our bedtime prayers. As I kissed her goodnight, I could see she looked sad, so I asked her why. She said, "Hey, Dad, you took Mommy on a date. But I didn't get a date."

So the next day, instead of me spending time preparing a sermon as I had planned, we went out on a daddy-daughter date. We got breakfast, drank hot chocolate, played cards, and went shopping. Throughout the day, as she had requests, she often began asking them by saying, "Hey, Dad." As we were heading home for the day, walking through the parking lot to the car, she was skipping along as happy as could be and singing a little impromptu song: "I love hanging out with my daddy!"

We got home, and at that point, I was very behind on sermon preparation, so I headed to my study and started to dig in. Our then six-year-old and two-year-old sons, Zac and Calvin, walked in together. "Hey, Dad," they said, "We wanna get a video game. Will you take us to get a video game?" I needed to work on my sermon, but I set it aside so we could hang out as guys and get the game they wanted.

Upon arriving home, Ashley informed me that she needed to go to the store by asking, "Hey, Dad, since you were going to get a haircut today, can I go with you, and we can also go to the store?" So we went to the store and got what she wanted.

By the time I started working on my sermon, the day was gone, and the kids were all in bed. Then it dawned on me how this relates to God as my Father. All day long, my kids were teaching me something about the Father heart of God. Their requests were reasonable and respectful. They just wanted to spend time with their dad and get help from their dad. And they didn't beg or whine or pester. They just asked me rather simply, and they began their requests with, "Hey, Dad," which is a lot like "Our Father."

I love my children and sometimes am frustrated that I am finite, with limits on the time I have, the energy I expend, and the resources I own. But "our Father in heaven" is inexhaustible. He is all-powerful, ever-present, and never overwhelmed, exhausted, or limited. How awesome is that?

Prayer happens naturally for people who realize that God is Father. Even more amazing, our Father rules and reigns over everyone and everything from His throne in heaven.

According to the storyline of the Bible, there is one reality in two realms. The seen realm is the physical world, where God's human family lives. The unseen realm is where God's divine family lives.[c]

Right now in the unseen realm our Father is present with the divine half of our family. Throughout the Bible, these divine beings are called angels, watchers, holy ones, hosts, the seat of the gods, the court in judgment, the host of heaven, the prince of the host, cherubim, seraphim, archangels, the commander, chief prince, lord, divine counsel, stars, morning stars, and sons of God. Occasionally the Bible gives us a glimpse into the unseen realm through the dreams or visions of people like Jacob, Daniel, Isaiah, and John. These revelations show us that the divine half of God's family is praying and worshipping

---

c My wife, Grace, and I wrote the book *Win Your War* for more information on spiritual warfare and the unseen realm.

in the unseen realm of heaven, just as the human half of God's family is praying and worshipping in the seen realm of earth.

Prayer, including worshipful singing, is a means of connecting these two realms. In some magnificent manner our prayers to our Father join their prayers to our Father. Revelation is John's glimpse into the unseen realm. In the presence of God he sees "golden bowls full of incense, which are the prayers of the saints. And they sang a new song."[d] John continues recording his vision, and a few chapters later he reports, "Another angel came and stood at the altar with a golden censer, and he was given much incense to offer with the prayers of all the saints on the golden altar before the throne, and the smoke of the incense, with the prayers of the saints, rose before God from the hand of the angel."[e]

Right now, in the presence of God are divine beings, departed human beings, and a bowl filled with your prayers. When you sing and pray, you are joining those who also call on "our Father" in the seen and unseen realm, accessing divine presence and also welcoming divine power.

Our Father is King! He rules over all times, all kings, all nations. He rules over all history: past, present, and future. Nothing is outside His authority. Our Father is the sovereign Creator and Lord of the universe. He is in control of all things.

This concept sometimes brings up a curious question. Some people may ask, "Well, if God is sovereign, why do I need to pray?" To me, this is like saying, "If your father is in charge, why would you talk to him and make requests of him?"

We pray *because* He's sovereign! We pray *because* He's in charge! We pray *because* He can help!

---

d Revelation 5:8–9
e Revelation 8:3–4

"Hallowed Be Your Name. Your Kingdom Come, Your Will Be Done, on Earth as It Is in Heaven": Worship

In any battle, secure and reliable communication channels are absolutely essential.[2]

In the ancient wars, Alexander, Hannibal, and Caesar used relay teams to carry messages to soldiers in battle and generals in command. Genghis Khan did the same but added homing pigeons to carry messages over battles. Eventually signal communication became popular, with hand motions and flags both on land and sea. Later, the electronic telegraph was invented along with Morse code. Modern technology, including the radio, telephone, airplane, television, computer, and internet all began, to some degree, as a military attempt at gaining communication advantage.

There are two kingdoms at war: the kingdom of lies and the kingdom of truth. There is the kingdom of death, and there is the kingdom of life. Disobedience and obedience are at war. Good and evil are doing battle.

Many people mistakenly think that there are two people in their relationship with God, but there are three. Your faith walk is not just you and God, but you and God and the enemy of you and your God. Not everything that happens is from God; there is plenty of evil and folly in the world. Sadly, every time something evil or foolish happens, some Christians blame God or people and overlook the possibility of spiritual warfare. This oversight is part of the great demonic deception.

Every day the prayers we pray, words we speak, and decisions we make either invite the kingdom of God down into our lives or pull the kingdom of hell up into our lives. The world we live in is the battlefield between these kingdoms in conflict, and prayer is our secure communication channel to the Father and our divine family, inviting their presence in our lives and battles. Satan and his demonic army can read the words we write and type, and hear the words we speak, but they cannot know the thoughts of our minds or longings of our heart because they are not God. In this way silent prayer is a private and secure communication channel for us to God.

The kingdoms of light and darkness are at war in this world, but one day our Father's kingdom will completely crush Satan and his kingdom with the arrival of the new heavens and the new earth. Until that day, however, we are to pray for our Father's kingdom to be made known in the earth through such things as love, peace, racial unity, forgiveness, and generosity for all, especially the poor and the marginalized.

Jesus did this by unleashing the Beatitudes, the opening declarations of the great kingdom blueprint we call the Sermon on the Mount. Jesus says that in God's kingdom, the mourners will be comforted, the meek get a generous inheritance, the hungry are well-fed, the merciful receive mercy, and so on. And He follows these declarations with the announcement that Christians are supposed to be preservers (salt) and witnesses (light) of this kingdom to the entire earth.

Because we are the Father's kids, we want to see this happen so that we can all finally be home and the war can finally be over. So we work and pray for this kingdom to show up and be made manifest on the earth. It begins with individuals and communities praying this will happen. As our hearts are stirred, we are then compelled to move our feet and use our hands to serve this kingdom.

Worship includes music and singing songs, but it is much more than this. It is also about living lives that do God's will.

Paul writes, "Therefore, I urge you, brothers and sisters, in view of God's mercy, to offer your bodies as a living sacrifice, holy and pleasing to God—*this is your true and proper worship.*"[f]

Worship is praying for the kingdom to come and then living as a citizen of that kingdom out of love for King Jesus. Prayer is how we align ourselves with God's will and position ourselves to help build God's kingdom.

Life is difficult. Jesus told us it would be. You might get cancer or lose your job. There's a good chance that you'll struggle, be abandoned, or be betrayed. And it's OK to ask God to fix it. But we must train ourselves to accept God's will and submit to it. It's a good thing to pray, "Your will be done," because it reveals our trust in God and acknowledges that His way is better and higher than our desires.

In prayer we tell God our will, but we ultimately seek His will. Sometimes prayer moves God's hands. Most of the time, prayer moves our hearts. God doesn't much need prayer, but we do. Prayer sometimes changes our circumstances so that we can get around hardship, but most of the time, prayer changes us so that we can get through our hardship.

> Sometimes prayer moves God's hands. Most of the time, prayer moves our hearts.

For our hearts to trust God above all else, we must begin worshipfully praying for our will to be aligned with His will. In every relationship we can find ourselves at a point of disagreement with someone. We sometimes refuse even to discuss the matter with them for the simple fact that we are not open to reconsidering our point of view. Once we are willing to sit down and

---

f Romans 12:1, NIV, EMPHASIS ADDED

discuss a point of disagreement with someone, we are opening ourselves up to having a change of mind.

Prayer does precisely this; it is our way of talking out a tough issue with God so that in the context of the loving relationship, we can come into agreement with God and have one vision for the future and walk forward together. Prayer is not how we come to have God do our will, but together with God, we agree on His will.

In some regards, prayer is how we verbally process things with God. For those of us who are verbal processors, we think with our mouths open. Since this is not always a good thing, a friend or spouse of a verbal processor lovingly goes through the process of listening and dialoguing, knowing that eventually the process will come to a conclusion

Prayer sometimes changes our circumstances so that we can get around hardship, but most of the time, prayer changes us so that we can get through our hardship.

and be worth the mess it can take to get there. We only make matters worse when we verbally process with the wrong people or vent online. Prayer is one way of verbally processing with the Lord so that in the end we arrive at the point of accepting God's will for our lives.

The life of faith is trusting God's will through this life until we see it one day at the end of this life. Old preachers were fond of an illustration to help make this point. They would say that life is like an old knitting loom. From under the loom, as you look up at the yarn, all you see is a mess of knots. But, as you look down on the loom from above, a glorious and carefully threaded tapestry emerges, and a beautiful picture can be seen.

When we pray, "Your will be done," we are acknowledging that our vantage point on this side of the loom is not the clearest. We are trusting that our Father on the other side of the loom is knitting something glorious together with the threads and knots of life, and one day we will sit with Him on the other side to see it and celebrate it.

"GIVE US THIS DAY OUR DAILY BREAD": PROVISION

Throughout any given day, a parent can expect their child to repeatedly ask them for a big meal, little snack, or something to drink. This kind of request is nothing burdensome, and good parents like to know when their child is hungry or thirsty so that they can provide for them. Not only are adults supposed to answer the practical requests of children, but we are also supposed to remember that we are the Father's kids and also let our requests be known to Him.

After adoration and worship, the third focus of the Lord's Prayer is provision. This portion of the prayer allows us to ask for practical things in life. "Do not be anxious about anything, but in everything by prayer and supplication with thanksgiving let your requests be made known to God."[g]

Sadly something called "prosperity theology" has encouraged some Christians to pray for their greed rather than their need. Jesus, who was homeless, poor, and put to death by a rich political leader who lived in a big house, is probably not eager to make everyone rich, powerful, and blessed with a big

---

g Philippians 4:6

house. There's a big difference between praying for our daily bread and asking God to give us everyone else's daily bread as well. Nonetheless, you need your daily bread, and the Father wants you to ask Him to provide.

Do you have needs? Bring them to "Our Father."

You need food to eat, water to drink, and a place to live. For those things to get paid for, you also need a job and sufficient health to work it. God knows you have these needs, and when you ask Him, you are building your relationship. Your needs are not a burden. You are a blessing to your Father, just as children are a blessing to their parents. Just as a child who brings their needs to a loving parent is building the relationship, the same is true of you as God's child.

Your Father loves you and cares for you and wants what's best for you. Furthermore, your Father has all the resources imaginable at His disposal. Pray. Ask.

Some people sadly think that prayer is solely a spiritual business. They won't pray over meals or ask for practical needs because they feel as if those things are unspiritual. But we are whole people with integrated lives just like Jesus who ate meals and paid taxes, and the Father is happy for us to bring our needs to Him.

Like the children of God in Exodus who received enough food to last one day at a time, in Jesus' day, the people receiving the instruction of the Lord's Prayer had to pray for their food daily. Most of us do not. We have access to grocery stores, refrigerators, pantries, food delivery folks, and drive-through windows to keep our bellies full.

As modern-day Americans, we live in the most abundant of lands in the most abundant of times. If praying for your daily bread makes little sense to you in this context, then pray for others who do not enjoy such abundance. Use this focus of the Lord's Prayer to pray for God's provision for those who are living in poverty, famine, and disease. Praying this way gives us a heart for those beyond ourselves, a concern for "the least of these."[h]

Praying for God's provision for others is yet another extension of praying for God's will to be done on earth as it is in heaven. And, it compels us to be generous and help fund ministries that help answer the prayers for others to receive their daily bread. Praying for daily bread also reminds us that everything we have comes from God.

A final thought about this part of the Lord's Prayer is that one way to thank God for His provision and generosity is to give sacrificially and fast. Prayer and fasting often work together like two oars in a boat. We often think we are in control of the "material" aspects of our lives. But fasting from food (and other things) shows us how physically needy we are, in addition to putting us in tune with our spiritual needs instead of focusing on food, technology, or other things as distractions or addictions. In the same way, praying daily for our physical needs humbles us and causes us to remember we could not survive one day without God's grace.

"Forgive Us Our Debts": Confession

The fourth focus of the Lord's Prayer is something that Jesus never prayed for Himself because He never needed to. Jesus was tempted in all ways as we are, but He never sinned. We, however, are another story entirely. This section of the prayer reminds us of our sinful state in the light of God's holiness, our debt to God. Both sins of *omission*—not doing what we should

---

h Matthew 25:31–46

do—and sins of *commission*—doing things we shouldn't do—are accruing debt to God.

Most of us are keenly aware of our financial debt. Our credit card statements, mortgage bills, and rent come due every month. These debts are always hanging over our heads.

But our spiritual debt is not as keenly felt. Imagine that God sent you a monthly statement that detailed your debt to Him. Now imagine that every month none of your past debt was repaid and the debt mountain of sin was continually growing. Now also imagine that at the bottom of the statement each month, it was clearly stated that those who failed to repay their entire debt would be sentenced to an eternal debtor's prison called hell.

Our debt to God is massive, and Jesus reminds us of that.

Unlike your credit card company, God allows a third-party payment plan. On the cross, when Jesus died in our place for our sins, He paid the debt of death that we owe. This part of the Lord's Prayer reminds us of our sinful state before God, and it reminds us that total forgiveness of our entire debt—past, present, and future—is available! Because our Father is forgiving, and because Jesus, our Big Brother, paid our entire debt, we need not trust in such religious efforts as reincarnation, karma, works, or purgatory to pay off our debt.

"Forgive us our debts" is an incredible acknowledgment of God's grace. God can and will forgive our entire spiritual debt. (And He has!) This reality welcomes us to pray for forgiveness with confidence and thanksgiving. God in Christ cancels and forgives our debt. Now we can simply, humbly, and frequently confess our sins to one another and our Father, knowing that, "if we confess our sins, he is faithful and just and to forgive us our sins and to cleanse us from all unrighteousness."[i]

If God already sees what we do and has forgiven us, why do we need to confess our sins to Him? Again, this is a question of our position in relation to God. If we fail to confess that we are sinners by nature and choice, we allow Satan to continue deceiving us to sin more. We pile up an even greater debt, which creates a division between God and us and ultimately strains our relationship with Him. This makes it hard to hear Him, hindering our prayers. If we instead humble ourselves and admit our wrongdoing, we make deposits into a trusting, loving relationship with Him, which welcomes Him to help us see our sin and walk away from it. Jesus already died for our sins. We don't need to condemn ourselves to suffer for them again by failing to accept His forgiveness. As the classic Christian hymn rightly sings, "Jesus paid it all!"[3]

"As We Also Have Forgiven Our Debtors": Intercession

I (Ashley) once met a young man in my college campus prayer tent who was very embittered against his father for abandoning him at a young age. He wasn't interested in a relationship with Jesus because he knew he would have to extend Jesus' forgiveness to his father, and this young man didn't want his father to "get away with" all the pain he had caused. He was unable to see how the heavenly Father could let this happen to him. But after I explained that God holds each person accountable for their sin and is perfectly just, he was able to see that the bitterness he had against his father was unnecessarily poisoning his own life.

---

i 1 John 1:9

We all sin, and we are all sinned against. And as we trust God for forgiveness of our sins, we ought to trust God to help us forgive others when they sin against us.

Forgiveness is a gift God gives to us, intending that we then share it with others. God's forgiven people should be godly, forgiving people. This truth does not mean that we ignore, diminish, or even excuse their sin. It doesn't mean we accept it or approve it. It doesn't mean that we trust them or that in the future we remain relationally close to them. Forgiveness takes one person, but reconciliation takes two, so all we can do is our part.

The Greek word most used for forgiveness quite literally means to let it go. In choosing to forgive, we are saying, "I wish God's best for you. I give up my right to seek vengeance or justice. I leave your future in God's hands."

The test of whether you have forgiven someone is blessing them.[j] When someone acts like an enemy and we forgive and bless them, we are treating them the way that God treated us when we were acting as His enemies.

Prayerful intercession for those who sin against us preserves us from becoming bitter. Bitter people become sad, lonely, unpleasant, joyless people. But when we ask God to help us forgive and then we "let it go" through forgiveness, we battle embitterment and refuse vengeance. When we are sinned against and forced to choose whether we will forgive, we are standing at a fork in the road and deciding if we will get bitter or get better.

> God's forgiven people should be godly, forgiving people.

---

j Matthew 5:44

Without forgiveness there can be no relationship. Unless God forgave us, none of us could have a relationship with Him. Without forgiveness, we cannot have a relationship with anyone, which is why Jesus connects "forgive us our debts" and "as we also have forgiven our debtors."[k] There is no way to be happy, healthy, or holy apart from being forgiven and forgiving others.

Aren't you glad God isn't embittered against you? Aren't you glad that right now God is not nursing a grudge toward you and plotting to harm you?

Isn't there profound freedom in knowing this good news?

Isn't it nice to know that on our worst days we can safely run to God rather than fearfully running from God?

Forgiven people should be forgiving people. "Be kind and compassionate to one another, forgiving each other, just as in Christ God forgave you."[l]

As parents we have to teach our kids to personalize the gospel like this from an early age. None of us come out of our mama's tummy naturally confessing, repenting, forgiving, or reconciling. Sadly, many adults don't know how to forgive and reconcile because they weren't raised to forgive and reconcile. You know, "Train up a child in the way he should go, and when he is old he will not depart from it"[m] is true even when parents do a lousy job. We have to train our kids to forgive.

As a young girl, I (Ashley) remember playing with a friend in a sandbox at our house while our parents were inside. She said something mean to me, and I responded by throwing sand in her eyes. Because I was stubborn, I proudly stayed outside as she ran into the house crying. I felt as if she deserved it, and I

---

k Matthew 6:12, NIV
l Ephesians 4:32, NIV
m Proverbs 22:6, NKJV

didn't want to apologize unless she apologized too, because she had started it. I presented this case to the parents when they rushed outside, and to my parents' dismay, I wasn't willing to say I was sorry.

My friend eventually got all the sand out of her eyes, and after thinking about it a bit more, later that day, we were both able to truly apologize and forgive each other. We even hugged to show our parents that it was all resolved. In this case, we were both victims of each other's sin, although mine looked worse than hers, so we both needed to apologize and forgive. It just took me a while to feel OK about apologizing and forgiving even if she did not.

I do not envy my parents trying to teach me to lovingly reconcile with those that I sinned against and had sinned against me. Even as young as I was, I was reluctant to forgive and move on (this is an easy case for total depravity). Thankfully they were persistent in prayer and helped me learn to build healthy relationships with forgiveness as a cornerstone.

Christians ought to be relentlessly dedicated to confession, to owning up to our sins. Real Christians use the Bible as a mirror that shows us our sin. Religious Christians use the Bible as binoculars to ignore their sin and focus on the sins of others. Once we accept how much God has forgiven us for, it becomes a lot clearer why we should forgive what others have done to us.

Sadly when we do not forgive, we pull demonic torment from the culture of hell into our lives, families, and churches. Satan and demons are never forgiven for anything by God and never forgive any of us for anything we do. The culture of heaven is one of forgiveness. The culture of hell is one of unforgiveness.

When we choose not to forgive, we are opening ourselves to the demonic.

> Be angry and do not sin; do not let the sun go down on your anger, and give no opportunity to the devil....And do not grieve the Holy Spirit of God....Let all bitterness and wrath and anger and clamor and slander be put away from you, along with all malice. Be kind to one another, tenderhearted, forgiving one another, as God in Christ forgave you.
> —EPHESIANS 4:26–27, 30–32

When we are sinned against, we can invite the Holy Spirit and culture of heaven into our lives through forgiveness. Or we can pull the demonic spirits and culture of hell up into our lives through bitterness. This explains why Jesus teaches us to pray for forgiveness and pray against the enemy and his evil.

"LEAD US NOT INTO TEMPTATION, BUT DELIVER US FROM EVIL": PROTECTION

Although I (Ashley) am small and not very strong, I have a confidence level akin to that of my dad's, which has sometimes gotten me into trouble. Before I was married, I enjoyed traveling alone. My dad always jokingly told me to watch the movie *Taken* before I would go on a solo trip, warning me that I could be putting myself in danger. I agreed with him, but I just naively thought I would be able to face whatever perils came my way. Thankfully I was never truly in danger, but after a few scary encounters, I realized that my parents were right. I did not need to continue to walk into unsafe situations in the name of adventure. I could have fun without being in danger or risking being tempted to do something foolish. Even as an adult, I still need my dad's guidance because evil, like gravity, can pull me toward folly.

Not all people are trustworthy. Not all places are safe. Not all experiences will grow you in your relationship with God.

Sin is real. The devil and his demons are real. The world is filled with evil and fraught with temptation. God's people cannot afford to be foolish or naive.

While we can and should pray defensively for forgiveness when we sin, we should also pray offensively—in advance—before temptation comes and evil lurks. Of course, our Father never tempts us to sin,[n] but in this portion of the Lord's Prayer, Jesus is saying that we should agree with God's desire that we not bow to temptation and enter into evil.

Praying that God would protect us from temptation is just another extension of praying for God's will to be done. It is saying, "God, I agree with You, and I don't want to walk away from You in disobedience."

Practically speaking, don't just pray reactively *after* you sin. Pray preemptively or proactively against sin so that you can surrender to God *before* you surrender to sin!

Reactive prayer is defensive, whereas proactive prayer is offensive. We pray offensively because we know that as followers of Jesus we will be attacked with temptation by Satan just as Jesus was. One Bible scholar writes:

> "Lead us not into temptation" does not imply "don't bring us to the place of temptation" or "don't allow us to be tempted."...Nor does the clause imply "don't tempt us" because God has promised never to do that anyway (Jas 1:13). Rather, in light of the probable Aramaic underlying Jesus' prayer, these words seem best taken as "don't let us succumb to temptation" (cf. Mark 14:38) or "don't abandon us to temptation." We do of course periodically succumb to

---

n James 1:13–14

temptation but never because we have no alternative (1 Cor 10:13). So when we give in, we have only ourselves to blame. The second clause of v. 13 phrases the same plea positively, "Deliver us from evil" (or "from the evil one" [NIV marg.], from whom all evil ultimately comes). This parallelism renders less likely the alternate translation of the first clause as "do not bring us to the test" ("test" is an equally common rendering of *peirasmos*) either as times of trial in this life or as final judgment. If we are praying for rescue from the devil, he is more likely tempting than testing us (cf. under 4:1). God tests us in order to prove us and bring us to maturity (Jas 1:2–4; 1 Pet 1:6–9). Such tests should not be feared, nor should we pray for God to withhold them.[4]

This portion of the Lord's Prayer, then, is not about asking God not to tempt us (because, again, He doesn't do that) but about asking God to bolster our faith, to give us the strength and courage to follow Him more lovingly, more closely, and more boldly when tempted. It is praying that God would grant us a life of repentance where we turn from sin and walk with Him.[o]

Finally, by praying in advance against evil and temptation, our minds are kept from deception, and our hearts are kept from pollution. When we stop praying against evil, especially the specific evils that we so easily give in to, unless we stay on guard in prayer, our minds find a way of making evil look less evil than it truly is. The desires of our hearts slowly start to turn from God to sin. We have all had this very experience, and after we fall into sinful evil, the ministry of the Holy Spirit shows us how this happened so that we can remember to keep praying against evil as Jesus told us to. Evil in this world is like gravity; it is an invisible but very real and powerful force

---

o Acts 11:18; 2 Timothy 2:25

seeking to pull us down until it takes us down. Prayer is how we invite the Holy Spirit to pull us up and deliver us from evil.

THE ALIGNMENT OF THE LORD'S PRAYER

In any concert the band always saves its biggest song for the grand finale and plays that hit with full enthusiasm to motivate the fans to sing along in full-throated unison. The same is true with the conclusion of the Lord's Prayer.

> For if you forgive others their trespasses, your heavenly Father will also forgive you, but if you do not forgive others their trespasses, neither will your Father forgive your trespasses.
>
> —MATTHEW 6:14–15

Getting God to do what we want is not the primary point of prayer. Jesus reminds us that the primary point of prayer is not to move God but to change us. Above all, praying prayers that follow the example of the Lord's Prayer requires a radical reorienting of our hearts and wills around the heart and will of God.

This type of prayer shifts our focus from ourselves to our Father, who is the solution for all our problems. Remember, prayer is not something our Father needs but something the Father knows we need. Prayer empties us of our prideful self-sufficiency and opens us up to Spirit-dependency.

Why is such a radical shift required to pray like Jesus when He gave us the Lord's Prayer?

Because you can't tell the Father you want His name to be hallowed if you are actively living a life that dishonors Him. You can't tell the Father you want His will to be done if you are actively disobeying His will. You won't ask the Father to supply your daily bread if you think you've earned everything on your own. You won't ask the Father to forgive you if you have no conviction of your sin and no desire for repentance. You won't ask the Father to forgive others if you are always trying to do to others what they've done to you in vengeance. And you won't ask the Father to keep you from temptation if your life is oriented around feeding your flesh and worshipping yourself.

The Lord's Prayer is an example of a prayer that aligns our will with God's. You've probably heard the expression, "If you talk the talk, you'd better walk the walk." Praying is the catalyst for walking the talk.

When you pray prayers like the Lord's Prayer with a heart open to transformation, it allows you to be part of our Father's plan for His will to be done on earth starting with us. It is foolish for us to pray this way—for our Father's name to be hallowed and His will to be done, for sinners to be forgiven, and for people to be fed and led out of evil temptation—if we are not willing to align ourselves with our Father. That's the only way to be part of the solution and an answer to someone else's prayer. Indeed, God will even use us as His sons and daughters to forgive people, feed people, and lead them out of sin as answers to their prayers. The Lord's Prayer reminds us that prayer is so much bigger than us, but our Father is so loving that He includes us in His plans to bless others as He has blessed us.

REFLECTION

1. Do you truly see God as our loving, perfect, caring, and present Father? Explain why or why not.

2. Do you truly believe that God fully forgives you for everything you have ever done or will ever do and that Jesus paid your debt in full? Express your thankfulness for His forgiveness.

3. Is there anyone that you have not truly forgiven and you need to get some time alone with God to work through a process whereby you can truly forgive them from the heart? If so, consider journaling about this process of forgiveness.

4. In what area(s) of your life do you need to be praying offensively or proactively against temptation and evil?

5. List any people you know who are praying for material provisions that you could help meet their needs.

Chapter 6

THE LORD'S GETHSEMANE PRAYER

Then Jesus went with them to a place called Gethsemane, and he said to his disciples, "Sit here, while I go over there and pray." And taking with him Peter and the two sons of Zebedee, he began to be sorrowful and troubled. Then he said to them, "My soul is very sorrowful, even to death; remain here, and watch with me." And going a little farther he fell on his face and prayed, saying, "My Father, if it be possible, let this cup pass from me; nevertheless, not as I will, but as you will." And he came to the disciples and found them sleeping. And he said to Peter, "So, could you not watch with me one hour? Watch and pray that you may not enter into temptation. The spirit indeed is willing, but the flesh is weak." Again, for the second time, he went away and prayed, "My Father, if this cannot pass unless I drink it, your will be done." And again he came and found them sleeping, for their eyes were heavy. So, leaving them again, he went away and prayed for the third time, saying the same words again. Then he came to the disciples and said to them, "Sleep and take your rest later on. See, the hour is at hand, and the Son of Man is betrayed into the hands of sinners. Rise, let us be going; see, my betrayer is at hand."
—MATTHEW 26:36–46

OUR FAMILY LIVES in the desert, where everything is barren and parched, with one exception. In a few places, you will find fresh water surrounded by exploding greenery and life. If you surveyed the landscape where we live, you would assume there was no water and no rivers. The truth is, many of the rivers are underground and invisible to our sight. On occasion one of the rivers flows up to the surface, revealing the life hidden just below the seen surface. The result is a garden that springs forth wherever a river bursts through the clay.

The climate Jesus lived in was a desert similar to ours. In the Garden of Gethsemane, He stopped to spend a night in prayer. Just as unseen rivers spring forth to reveal life, so too Jesus taught us that the words on our lips flow from the deep rivers of our hearts: "What you say flows from what is in your heart."[a]

What flows from your heart on the last day of your life is the deepest water. The most important day of your life is your last day. Your first birthday, first day of school, and first day of marriage are all major milestones worth celebrating. The last day of life, however, is by far your most important day.

For some people, their last day comes on them suddenly and unexpectedly. For others, their last day comes on them slowly and painfully.

As Jesus approached the end of His last day, He stopped to spend an entire night in prayer. What someone does in the final moments of their life reveals who or what they care most about. Jesus' actions reveal that meeting with the Father in prayer was His highest priority.

Reading Jesus' Gethsemane prayer is spiritually overwhelming, just as it was physically overwhelming for Jesus. His

---

a Luke 6:45, NLT

tear-stained, agonizing prayer is a sacred glimpse into His most miserable moment so that He might comfort us on our darkest days.

Jesus' prayer in the darkness of the garden is brutally and painfully honest. In His darkest hour of abandonment and betrayal, with the horrid specter of crucifixion quickly coming, Jesus did not doubt the Father, deny the Father, rebel against the Father, or run from the Father. No, instead, He got down on His knees in surrender to speak with the Father in prayer. In this act we witness another reminder of one of the great truths about prayer: it is not primarily about getting God to do what we want but rather having our will aligned with His. That way, when the most brutal moments of life envelop us, we will take the Father's hand to lead us through—and not around—our valleys of darkness.

> *What someone does in the final moments of their life reveals who or what they care most about.*

THE ROAD TO THE GARDEN

In the chapters leading up to Matthew 26, Jesus begins warning His followers of His impending death. "I will be handed over," He says. "I will be betrayed."

Jesus was fully aware of where His ministry was going, foretelling the manner of His murder. The only thing worse than marching into a deadly assault is knowing the outcome well in advance and marching forward anyway.

> From that time Jesus began to show his disciples that he must go to Jerusalem and suffer many things from the

elders and chief priests and scribes, and be killed, and on the third day be raised.

—MATTHEW 16:21

Jesus said to them, "The Son of Man is about to be delivered into the hands of men, and they will kill him, and he will be raised on the third day." And they were greatly distressed.

—MATTHEW 17:22–23

And as Jesus was going up to Jerusalem, he took the twelve disciples aside, and on the way, he said to them, "See, we are going up to Jerusalem. And the Son of Man will be delivered over to the chief priests and scribes, and they will condemn him to death and deliver him over to the Gentiles to be mocked and flogged and crucified, and he will be raised on the third day."

—MATTHEW 20:17–19

Jesus' tone grows dark and His words ominous as His preaching emphasizes the sober subjects of sin, judgment, hell, and heaven, which are all the issues at hand as He heads to the cross. It is in this season that Judas Iscariot agrees to betray his Master. He receives Jesus' love, hears Jesus' teaching, and receives Jesus' provision, but like so many today, He learned about the Lord but never loved the Lord, much like Satan, who possessed him. As we enter Matthew's twenty-sixth chapter, Judas decides to stab Jesus in the front with a kiss on the face and, fulfilling the prophecy of Zechariah 11:12–13, agrees to sell Jesus out for thirty pieces of silver.

While Jesus is eating dinner with His disciples at Simon the leper's house,[b] a woman enters and lavishly anoints Jesus in a profound act of worship. His friends object, but Jesus waves them off to receive her gift, which He calls beautiful. Jesus was

---

b Matthew 26:6–13

118

then able to smell the ointment from that alabaster flask, the offering of this poor woman's appreciation, throughout His betrayal and murder. Later, as He hung on the cross, the lingering scent would serve as a reminder that His life was also a sweet fragrance poured out as an act of worship.

Jesus would have smelled her worship and repentance through His prayer for perseverance. Her generous sacrifice of worship likely encouraged Jesus to give His life as the ultimate sacrifice of worship. He endured it all with the scent of her need for a Savior as a reminder. "Christ loved us and gave himself up for us as a fragrant offering and sacrifice to God."[c]

The death of Jesus was shrouded in the Passover season. All God's people, in keeping with the scriptural commands instituted in the days of Moses, would gather to deal with their sin before God in faith that one day their Messiah would come to shed His blood in their place for salvation from sin.[d] In the days leading up to the Israelites' exodus from slavery in Egypt, God sent an array of plagues to accompany Moses' demands to Pharaoh. The plague that broke the back of Egypt was the killing of the firstborn sons.[e] Every family was to apply the blood of a spotless lamb to their doorpost in faith of God's deliverance. Any family that did not have the mark of blood on their household would lose their firstborn son to death. God instituted blood sacrifice as the means of grace, and from that point on, God's people celebrated this event as a lasting ordinance, commemorating His wrath and forgiveness with the Passover feast. Our faith is to be two things:

1. Private—in our homes as worship to our God

---

c Ephesians 5:2
d 1 Corinthians 5:7
e Exodus 12

2. Public—outside our homes as a witness to our neighbors

Jesus and His disciples ate their final Passover meal together[f] —what we now call the Last Supper—and the meal took a dark turn when Jesus revealed that one of those present at the table with Him would betray Him. Jesus knew in His heart that it would be Judas, His pretend friend. Shortly after that, Peter, appointed to be the next singular head of the ministry, pledged never to betray Jesus. Yet Jesus revealed to Peter that he too would deny his Lord. Jesus was keenly aware that His journey to the cross would be paved with betrayal and abandonment until He was utterly alone.

Nevertheless, Jesus invited His nearest and dearest disciples to partner with Him in prayer to prepare for the pain. He sets an example for us to invite those we love into our darkest days and not be shocked if they fail to walk with us through our valley of the shadow of death. After the meal, Jesus went with them to Gethsemane, and He said to them, "Sit here while I go over there and pray." He walked a little further with Peter, James, and John, and He said to them, "My soul is very sorrowful, even to death; remain here, and watch with me." Then Jesus walked a little further by Himself and "fell on his face" and cried out to God in history's most painful prayer.[g]

THE GARDEN

Gethsemane means an oil press, and an oil press stood amid a field of olive trees, where it was used to press the oil from the fruit by crushing it. John 18:1 reveals that an olive grove,

---

f Matthew 26:17–29
g Matthew 26:36–39

or garden, was in this place where Jesus prayed. There, Jesus' soul would be pressed until it was crushed and heartfelt prayer poured forth.

It is not coincidental that Jesus ended up in this garden. It is a pivotal point in history, and it is pivotal for its connection to a previous pivotal moment in a garden. Just as Adam faced a choice between obedience and disobedience in the Garden of Eden and failed, Jesus faced the choice in the Garden of Gethsemane.[h]

The first Adam turned from the Father in a garden; the last Adam turned to the Father in a garden. The first Adam was naked and unashamed; the last Adam was naked and bore our shame. The first Adam's sin brought us thorns; the last Adam wore a crown of thorns. The first Adam substituted himself for God; the last Adam was God substituting Himself for sinners. The first Adam sinned at a tree; the last Adam bore our sin on a tree. The first Adam died as a sinner; the last Adam died for sinners. Adam fell to sin in a garden, but Jesus fell to His knees in a garden to ensure that He did not fall prey to sin.

The night road to the Garden of Gethsemane was dark. Foreboding, it was littered with the heartbreak of betrayal and abandonment. The air was thick with pain and angst. At that moment, the weight of the world came on Jesus. He carried the sin of humanity to the cross, to the Place of the Skull looming on the horizon.

Maybe you know what it's like to see that devastating moment just hanging over you. Have you had your Gethsemane moment? Were you overwhelmed by what was happening to you, feeling lonely because of abandonment and betrayal,

---

h Romans 5:12–21; 1 Corinthians 15:45

helpless to change your fate and sensing there was no way you were going to make it?

In His moment of dying, Jesus didn't distrust, doubt, deny, or disregard God. Instead, He desired God. *So He prayed.*

"SIT HERE, WHILE I GO OVER THERE AND PRAY"

Even Jesus needed to pray!

When you are sick, lonely, hurting, and in need, you need to talk to God. Even sinless, perfect Jesus needed to talk to the Father. If Jesus needed to pray in His Gethsemane moment, you need to pray in yours.

Jesus was at a place of utter submission—totally overcome by the pain of the burden He was to bear in place of sinners to be their Savior. Jesus was so anguished that His sweat was like drops of blood.[i] This prayer is not pithy; it's painful.

Sweating blood is an extreme medical condition only possible for those experiencing the most devastating distress humanly possible. Very few people ever get to this point.

Jesus was devastated, mournful, and anguished. It's OK to be devastated, mournful, and anguished. There are times for those feelings. Not all anxiety is sin.

The question is: What do you do in those moments?

When your spouse says, "I'm leaving," when the doctor says, "It's cancer," when the nurse says, "You've miscarried," when your siblings say, "Dad died, and he didn't know Jesus," what do you do? What you don't need to do on those days is pretend. Don't pretend that life is easy and life is good. It's OK to say life is complicated and sometimes very, very painful.

Jesus is sorrowful until the point of death (Matt. 26:38). He is beyond sad. He is devastated, and His soul is wounded. He is

---

i Luke 22:44

sweating blood. The situation is awful, horrible, and unavoidable. Jesus is emotionally present in the haunting moment, fully experiencing its horror.

It is sad that the theology of some people does not work when they need it most. If your theology is that Christians are happy, what happens when you're grieving? If you believe that Christians are winners, what happens when you lose? If you believe that Christians are healthy, what happens when you are sick? If your theology teaches that Christians are rich, what happens when you are poor? If you believe that Christians are always victorious, what happens when you are defeated?

We should love the brutal honesty of the Scriptures. God became a man, and He goes where we go. He goes to the cross, and that path is paved with betrayal and sadness and loneliness and grief marked by a trail of tears mixed with blood.

And if He went where we go, then we should go where He went in our Gethsemane griefs: on our face in prayer to the Father.

"Not as I Will, but as You Will"

Jesus begins His Gethsemane prayer with these haunting words: "My Father, if it be possible, let this cup pass from me; nevertheless, not as I will, but as you will."[j]

That cup is wrath.

In this first of three prayers in the garden, Jesus humbly and earnestly made His request known that He preferred that the cup of suffering and wrath be taken from Him. While there is some debate among biblical commentators regarding Jesus' mention of the "cup," it seems best, based on the context of its

---

j Matthew 26:39

appearance throughout the Old Testament, to identify the cup as God's wrath poured out on sinners as if from a cup.[k]

Every moment of every day, sinners continue rebelling while thinking they are getting away with everything. The truth is, sinners get away with nothing but instead store up everything: "But because of your hard and impenitent heart you are storing up wrath for yourself on the day of wrath when God's righteous judgment will be revealed."[l] The word picture is sobering. Imagine in God's presence an uncountable number of cups, each with a person's name on it. Every time they sin, their cup of wrath fills up more and more. God's holy justice demands that every cup be emptied in one of two ways:

1. You drink your cup of God's wrath forever in hell.

2. You trust that Jesus drank your cup of God's wrath on the cross, which was His hell.

Jesus did not fear physical death so much as He dreaded the loss of relationship with God the Spirit and God the Father as He took our place and emptied our cup of God's wrath, drinking every last drop. Jesus knew that by going to the cross, He took on our sin and stood condemned in our place, dying as our substitute. He knew that the Father's wrath would be poured out on him and that for the first and only time in all eternity, He would be separated from the Father and the Spirit—totally abandoned and handed over to endure wrath alone.[m]

What Jesus' holds in the highest regard is the same thing we should—an intimate, warm personal relationship with God.

---

k Psalm 11:6; Isaiah 51:17; Ezekiel 23:33
l Romans 2:5
m 2 Corinthians 5:21

Jesus is saying, in essence, "Father, if Your wrath can be taken from Me and My relationship with You can be unbroken, I would prefer that."

Nevertheless, Jesus favors the Father's will, not His own.

This difference is the distinction between pagan prayer and Christian prayer. Pagan prayer insists that we can make God do what we want. In pagan prayer God is a vending machine, and with the right prayer, or by praying with enough "faith," we can hit a button and force God to grant our request.

"*My* will be done" is the mark of pagan prayer. "*Your* will be done" is the mark of Christian prayer. It is another way of saying, "I am not the lord of my life."

In the final hours of their lives, it was Judas who kissed Jesus in total dishonesty and Jesus who prayed in total honesty. "You can trust a friend who corrects you, but kisses from an enemy are nothing but lies."[n] The truth is, like Jesus, you are going to be betrayed, be lonely, feel overwhelmed, and see your body fail and life end. Jesus promised us we'd have trouble in this world.[o] Will you act like Judas or Jesus when that day comes?

Our prayer is that you will call out to God, making your requests known humbly and respectfully and honestly, and that you will say submissively, "Not my will. Your will, God." Prayer is about God changing us, not about us changing God.

God is sovereign, and God is good. When you pray for the Father's will, you are saying in faith, "You are in charge, God, not me. And You know what is best, not me. Even if I don't understand, I will wrestle with You so that I can come to agree with You because our relationship is more important than any issue."

---

n Proverbs 27:6, CEV
o John 16:33

We often don't know what's going on. All we see is our narrow view of life clouded by our circumstances. We do not have God's all-knowing vantage point. The prophet asks us, "Who has measured the spirit of the LORD, or what man shows him his counsel?"[p] No one can raise their hand to provide an answer.

At the close of His first prayer, Jesus the Son is affirming the glorious truth of God the Father's perfect sovereignty and sub-mitting to it when He utters one of the most significant state-ments in all Scripture regarding prayer: "As you will."[q] This refrain is the correct attitude for every child of God worship-ping in prayer. Prayer is where we make our requests known to God and then ask Him not only to have His way but also to transform us so that our way matches His. We might not start there, but we get there by praying until we pray the surrender prayer, "as You will."

> Prayer is about God changing us, not about us changing God.

The fact that Jesus reveals His will to God the Father has caused lots of theological speculation. One Bible commentator writes:

> Here then appears the classic scriptural example of a prayer that God does not answer in the way desired by the one praying, yet without any fault in the person making the request. Here, too, is a key reminder for us. If Christ could plead as boldly as he did, we should feel free also to unload all our deepest desires before God (esp. in light of Ps 37:4). Yet we dare not blame ourselves or others if we do not receive what we ask for when we have asked with right

p Isaiah 40:13
q Matthew 26:39

motives (Jas 4:3). If Christ had to guard his own requests with this type of qualification...how dare we ever try to pray for anything without also adding "if it be your will"!¹

The scholar goes on to explain that the anguish of Jesus' Gethsemane prayer means that godly people can and do experience anxiety that causes depression: "A further application emerges from Jesus' sorrow. His depression means 'that all depression is not sin...in fact, nothing is more unhelpful than telling people in very sad circumstances not to be depressed.'"²

Looking back on Jesus' Gethsemane prayer, it is said:

> In the days of his flesh, Jesus offered up prayers and supplications, with loud cries and tears, to him who was able to save him from death, and he was heard because of his reverence. Although he was a son, he learned obedience through what he suffered.ʳ

If our Lord Jesus Christ in His full humanity struggled to come into agreement with the Father's will for His life without sinning, then this must mean that we have the same freedom. Jesus did come around into full surrender to the Father's will but only after a lot of tears and prayers.

Any good parent knows something about this reality. At some point every child has a fear of something they are facing, and the parent has two choices. One, they can remove the obstacle before the child so that they do not have to deal with it. Two, they can lovingly and patiently talk with, listen to, comfort, and reassure the child that they will get through it. We are the Father's kids, and the example of our Jesus, our big brother, is that our dad invites us to be honest in prayer, and

---

r Hebrews 5:7–8

He will help us come to the place where we do not simply obey against our will but surrender our will to His in faith.

Jesus, in His full humanity, benefited from the comfort of an angel sent to strengthen Him during the Gethsemane prayer.[s] Therefore, we should be comforted to know that when we pray our Gethsemane prayers, it is Jesus who intercedes for us, bringing our request to the Father and sending the Spirit to strengthen us.

"THE SPIRIT IS WILLING, BUT THE FLESH IS WEAK"

Jesus finishes His first prayer and briefly returns to His friends: "And he came to the disciples and found them sleeping. And he said to Peter, 'So, could you not watch with me one hour? Watch and pray that you may not enter into temptation. The spirit indeed is willing, but the flesh is weak.'"[t]

In His moment of greatest need, Jesus' friends left Him alone and fell asleep. It is easy to judge them but don't. They are us. We are them.

Has God ever caught you being lazy? Have you ever been caught sleeping on the job, spiritually speaking? Have you been guilty of fruitless faith? Who among us hasn't ever failed to be a faithful friend to Jesus? When we read the Bible, it can be tempting to put ourselves in the position of Jesus and see the failures of others toward us. But before we use the Bible as binoculars to see their sin, we need to use it as a mirror to see our sin. Every one of us has *had* friends like Jesus' friends and *been* friends like Jesus' friends.

Maybe it's not a direct evil you've committed; maybe it's a

---

s Luke 22:43
t Matthew 26:40–41

sin of omission. You're not doing what you ought. In any event, this scene only illustrates what is true for all of us: Jesus is perfectly faithful even when we are persistently faithless.

We are perhaps most tempted toward spiritual laziness—tempted to give up on prayer—when we believe God is taking too long. Maybe the disciples didn't know Jesus needed that much time. But sometimes large problems need long prayers! Earlier in the book, we advised against praying too long, but the bigger the anguish, the longer you will need. The majority of the psalms are rather short, but some are pretty long. Don't short shrift prayer in times of intense suffering and pain. You have God's permission to be devastated.

Do you have cancer? Are you being cheated on? Did your child just die?

Pray! And pray with endurance, as a person fleeing from wildfire who has to run many miles before finding a safe place. Gethsemane prayers are like that. They are anxious and exhausting and can take a while.

Weakness is a fact of life. These dismal disciples are Jesus' small group of best friends. Let us just say this to you: If your friends aren't always there for you, if your friends sometimes bail on you, if your friends tend to fail to pray for you, congratulations, you have biblical friendships. Welcome to the real Christian life as experienced by Christ. The only perfect Christian is Christ, and He is faithfully and patiently working on the rest of us Christians.

The disciples learned to take care of one another because they first failed to take care of Jesus. They later became amazing pastors and preachers, but they learned from having been lazy, forgetful disciples.

Humble prayer reminds us of this. We are weak, but God is

strong, and His strength is perfected in our weakness. That's good news for those us with bad résumés.

Jesus likely knew that His friends would fail, but He nevertheless invited His friends to wake up and help Him out. After less than an hour in the anguish of prayer, He found them not praying for Him as He needed. This solitude is another aspect of Jesus' painful prayer. We witness here the utter loneliness Jesus suffered in His hour of greatest need as His friends succumbed to sleep rather than prevailing in prayer alongside Him.

"YOUR WILL BE DONE"

Jesus returns to His prayer, picking up where He left off: "Again, for the second time, he went away and prayed, 'My Father, if this cannot pass unless I drink it, your will be done.'"[u]

Why this prayer a second time? It's not because God didn't hear Him.

It is because Jesus felt it deeply. It is because He was reminding Himself! Sometimes we pray the same things over and over not to convince God but to submit that need continually to God's sovereign care.

Once more Jesus earnestly wrestles in prayer with the Father's will for Him to atone for the sins of the world to make enemies into family. While earnestly making His pain and sorrow known to the Father, Jesus again submits His will to the Father's, saying, "Your will be done," which is the deepest prayer anyone can ever pray. This painful prayerful of surrendered submission reveals the importance of praying for God to move *us* rather than us praying to move God.

---

u Matthew 26:42

You pray for your desires, offering them to God. And you pray that God's will be done.

Christianity is not designed to be risk-averse. The Christian religion is not designed to get you around your Gethsemane. It is a relationship with Jesus, who went through His Gethsemane and gets you through your Gethsemane. Jesus is a friend who won't fall asleep on you or fail to pray for you, as He lives to make intercession.

I (Mark) will never forget one of my first pastoral calls. Every hospital visit I'd done up to that point had been to help celebrate the birth of a healthy baby. They're chubby, and they're cute. You ask to hold them, you smile for a picture, and you pray. Amen. You're done. Yay, God!

Suddenly I was on my first hospital call that was not like that at all. A husband came home to find that his young and seemingly healthy bride was on the floor of their apartment unresponsive. The young husband called the medics, who rushed the woman to the hospital. He met me in the hallway saying something to the effect of, "They say she is brain dead, but her body is not yet dead. They want me to pull the plug. She's in a lot of pain. I don't know what to do. I don't know how I feel about pulling her life support, but I can't stand to see her die slowly in such agony. Will you pray with me?"

Of course, I said yes. But what do we pray?

I remember sitting in the hospital lobby with my face in my hands, praying James 1:5 for wisdom over and over. We prayed that God would heal her. We prayed long and hard. We prayed with tears in our eyes.

And then her husband said to God, "Your will be done."

Then his young wife died. He did not pretend to understand why death came so quickly after their honeymoon, but he invited Jesus to be with him, pray for him, and get him through his Gethsemane. And Jesus proved to be a faithful friend.

At her funeral he thanked God that she loved Jesus, that their few short years together were blessed, and that He would enjoy their friendship forever one day. He felt this loss in his soul, he mourned this loss for months and years, and he trusted in the will of God, even using his pain to preach the good news of Jesus Christ, who forgives sin and defeats death, to everyone who would listen.

Another time, I went to the hospital to see a friend's newborn twin boys. One was healthy, and one was sick. One was strong, and the other was weak. Their mother—a sweet, godly lady—said, "Pastor Mark, can you pray?"

We prayed for healing, for strength, for recovery.

And she said to God, "Your will be done."

One baby died. The other baby lived.

With tears in their eyes and sobbing so deep they could barely breathe, this godly young couple gave thanks at the funeral that God was willing to give His only Son to forgive sin, defeat death, and provide hope beyond the grave. Their response in their Gethsemane reminded me a lot of Jesus'.

Are you willing to go there with God? Are you willing to *live* there with God?

It's OK to pray, "I'm single, and I'd like to be married," if you also pray, "Your will be done."

It's OK if you're married to pray for a child if you also pray, "Your will be done."

It's important to pray that God would keep our marriages strong and faithful. And when someone commits adultery, it is important to pray for repentance and change of heart and reconciliation. But it's also important to pray, "Your will be done," because change of heart and reconciliation don't always happen.

I know a guy who worked very hard to provide for his family. He loved them very much, consistently and sacrificially. He got up early every morning to work so his wife could be home with their kids. He discipled his kids and prayed with them.

He came home early one day, saw another car in his driveway, and walked in to find his wife in bed with another man while his kids played in the basement. He later found out that a parade of men had been through his home while he was at work and attending a men's Bible study.

Can you imagine how his world might shatter in those moments? Maybe you can because you've been there. Suddenly he's having doubts about whether all the kids are his. He is in a place of not only shock but utter devastation.

"Pastor Mark," he says, "what am I supposed to pray?"

Pray for a changed heart because she probably doesn't know Jesus. Pray you don't have a disease. Pray that the kids are all yours. Pray that she will repent. Pray that you will be able to forgive her.

But pray, "Father, not my will but Your will be done."

God doesn't always make it "all better," at least not in this life. God can and does answer prayer. Sometimes He even gets you out of Gethsemane. But sometimes He just gets you through it.

God writes the story we call our life.

The first lie told to our first parents included the illusion that we, and not God, can decide what is good and is evil. Every day since, we have needed to walk humbly and not assume that we would make a good god.

Jesus, in a moment of deep anguish and abandonment, prays three times for more than an hour, sweating blood in distress and desire for the Father's will. That's the Christian life of suffering and surrender through painful prayer.

When Christ said to take up your cross to follow Him and deny yourself, this is what He meant.

"Your will be done."

If you believe God is good, pray, "Your will be done." If you believe God knows better than you, pray, "Your will be done." If you believe God loves you, pray, "Your will be done." And if you cannot pray, "Your will be done," then just keep praying until you can.

"FOR THE THIRD TIME, SAYING THE SAME WORDS AGAIN"

As the story in the garden continues, again, Jesus' disciples (which we also are) were consistently faithless, while Jesus was persistently faithful. "And again he came and found them sleeping, for their eyes were heavy."[v] They've conked out on Him again. Despite His repeated request, Jesus' disciples again failed Him, as each of His disciples has ever since.

Jesus does not rebuke them but instead heads to the cross to redeem them, "So, leaving them again, he went away and prayed for the third time, saying the same words again."[w] Rather than arguing with people, Jesus was praying with the Father.

He prayed a third time, the same prayer, "My Father, if it be

v Matthew 26:43
w Matthew 26:44

possible, let this cup pass from me; nevertheless, not as I will, but as you will."ˣ

That is how deeply His pain was felt. That's how anguished He was. He cried out to heaven for His life while preparing for His death.

The subtle implication is not that Jesus merely prayed the same prayer three times but that he *only* prayed it three times. He simply didn't have enough time to pray it any longer.

Some suffering has a known expiration date like Jesus' suffering, but some seems to go on endlessly. I (Ashley) have struggled with mysterious back and stomach pain since I was very young, and I have spent much time crying out to God, asking why I suffer in this way. At times I physically feel at my limit as I go to the hospital yet again or start a new treatment plan in hopes of healing, and spiritually I get discouraged as well.

The question of God's sovereignty and goodness amid suffering is a popular and valid one, but when seeking an answer, we must keep in mind that Jesus suffered most of all. He was betrayed, forsaken, martyred, ridiculed, and mocked—and He was God. Like Jesus, our lives have a purpose in God's eyes, and the Father's timing is perfect. Praying in a way that invites the kingdom down helps fix our eyes on eternity, like Jesus, who knew that the cross was not the end of His story.

THE ROAD OUT OF THE GARDEN

Back in the garden, Jesus "came to the disciples and said to them, 'Sleep and take your rest later on. See, the hour is at

---

x Matthew 26:39

hand, and the Son of Man is betrayed into the hands of sinners. Rise, let us be going; see, my betrayer is at hand.'"[y]

Jesus' disposition has changed. He has laid His heart out to the Father. He's said His piece and made His peace. He has approached the throne boldly in His time of need. He has submitted His will to the Father's. Jesus resolved that the only thing worse than dying for the sin of the world is not living in the Father's will.

Resolved and committed to the will of the Father now as He had always been, Jesus rouses His sleeping friends and prepares to be kissed by Satan through His pretend friend Judas. This act fulfills King David's prophecy given roughly a thousand years prior: "Even my close friend in whom I trusted, who ate my bread, has lifted his heel against me."[z]

Have you ever been betrayed by a close friend? Jesus knows your pain. Judas had seen Jesus walk on water, heal lepers, raise the dead, love on children, and never wrong anyone in His entire life and ministry, and yet he was still willing to sell out the sinless Son of God for a few bucks. Have you been there? Have you poured out your life for someone, sacrificed for them, loved them to your limit, only to have them stab you in the front while they look you in the eye? Jesus has.

Jesus was falsely arrested, accused, tried, and condemned. Jesus was brutally flogged, His flesh violently ripped from His body. He suffered unspeakable agony. Jesus was crucified while people jeered, cursed, spat on, and mocked Him for claiming to be a king, while blood flowed from His crown of thorns down His beaten body as His mother watched in horror. And

---

y Matthew 26:45–46
z Psalm 41:9

if all that wasn't horrendous enough, Jesus, who knew no sin, took our sin on Himself and put His righteousness on us.[aa]

Jesus was then abandoned not only by His friends but also by God the Father; God the Father turned His back on God the Son for the first and only time in human history. Jesus used His final breaths to pray for the forgiveness of sinners before committing His spirit to God the Father and breathing His last. The sequence of events leading up to the cross reveals to us that Jesus "for the joy that was set before him endured the cross, despising the shame."[ab]

Jesus accepted a death He didn't deserve so that we might avoid a death we do deserve.

Betrayal, torture, abandonment, and death—Jesus' prayer didn't get Him *around any of it*. He drank every drop of it. But prayer got Him through it. He endured it.

If you're a Christian, you pray to get around it, but you also pray, "Your will be done." And if you must go through it, you'll be ready. It'll hurt like hell, but you'll be with Jesus, and you'll become like Jesus, and you'll have the joy of Jesus because you will be in the will of God.

Had Jesus not endured this, we would all go to hell. Every one of us would be kindling stacked up for an eternal bonfire of the condemned. There'd be no forgiveness, no salvation for sin. He laid down what was easiest for Him and endured what was best for us. This sacrifice is the apex of great commandment obedience. "Greater love has no one than this," Jesus tells us, "that someone lay down his life for his friends."[ac] Jesus is a friend like no other.

Submitting to the Father's will to the point of death for a

---

aa 2 Corinthians 5:21
ab Hebrews 12:2
ac John 15:13

sinful world, Jesus gives up His last breath and dies, going to be reconciled back to the Father. His battered, lifeless body is torn from the cross. He is buried.

Three days later, Jesus roars back to life. For forty days, He appears to His followers and crowds of up to five hundred. Jesus was back in the pulpit! He began to give them final instructions before His ascension. What did He teach?

The Gethsemane prayer.

We know this because nobody was there to hear Him pray this three-fold prayer. He was alone, and His disciples were asleep. So, He shared the details of those moments with them, teaching His prayer to them. It was so important that He wanted His followers to know what He prayed, how He felt, and what He said so we could learn from it and pray like it.

> Death is real, sin is real, evil is real, and pain is real.

It is an extraordinary, powerful truth that we don't have a high priest who is unable to sympathize with our weaknesses.[ad] In our world of suffering and strife, death and defeat, it is impossible to worship a God who refused to enter into this world to sympathize with us.

Death is real, sin is real, evil is real, and pain is real.

These things are true. But do you know what else is true?

God is real, salvation is real, forgiveness is real, and healing is real.

In your Garden of Gethsemane moments when you feel alone, desperate, hurting, afflicted, and empty, we trust you will find our good, gracious, loving God to care for you. In

---

ad Hebrews 4:15

your moments of anguished prayer, He is there, comforting you, holding you as you walk through the darkness out to the other side. He might not steer you around the valley of the shadow of death, but He will walk through the valley with you. He is God over that valley, He is Lord over all shadows, and He is certainly sovereign over death. He is God, and He is good.

Friend, His kingdom will come, and His will *will* be done. Like Jesus, you need to keep pushing forward through your valley of the shadow of death with your King until you see His kingdom on the other side.

> God is real, salvation is real, forgiveness is real, and healing is real.

REFLECTION

There are eleven things the Gethsemane prayer stresses on us, things we can learn from Jesus' prayer. There are innumerable other lessons we can learn from the prayer in addition to these eleven, but we pose these application questions as points of prayerful examination, meditation, and discussion.

1. Do you pray to get from God or to get God?

2. Do you pray for God to move or for God to move you?

3. Can your friends count on you to persevere in prayer for them?

4. Describe any situation in your life where you struggle to pray, "Your will be done."

5. In your life, what has been your Gethsemane moment(s)?

Chapter 7

PRAY FOR YOURSELF

The Lord's High Priestly Prayer, Part 1

When Jesus had spoken these words, he lifted up his eyes to heaven, and said, "Father, the hour has come; glorify your Son that the Son may glorify you, since you have given him authority over all flesh, to give eternal life to all whom you have given him. And this is eternal life, that they know you, the only true God, and Jesus Christ whom you have sent. I glorified you on earth, having accomplished the work that you gave me to do. And now, Father, glorify me in your own presence with the glory that I had with you before the world existed."
—JOHN 17:1–5

SINCE GRACE AND I (Mark) started a church before our oldest child, Ashley, was born, our kids have literally spent their entire lives in ministry. Like all families, we have rowed through some rough seas together.

One season of our lives felt more like a hurricane. The skies were dark, waves were fierce, and danger was overwhelming. You know what these seasons of life are like, as we've all had them.

Eventually the hurricane subsided, the sun came out, the waves died down, and smooth sailing thankfully resumed.

God kindly had us relocate to Scottsdale, Arizona, to heal up, rest up, and get time together with our Father and our family. I remember one particular time when we sat outside together, eating dinner on a picturesque warm winter night as a sunset lit up the clear sky. I felt compelled in the Spirit to ask the family whether there was anything they were burdened by during our stormy season that they were still carrying.

One of the younger children said, "Dad, it's just nice to have you back."

This one line revealed a much bigger issue that I needed to investigate. So I said, "Thank you for sharing that. I really love you, and it would help your dad if you could explain what you mean while I listen."

They said, "Well, when things were really bad, you were physically present with us, but you were emotionally absent. I knew you loved us, but you were often overwhelmed, busy, and stressed out, and so in some ways, you were not present."

As heartbreaking as it was to hear this as a dad, I knew it was true. Wanting to probe further as the family listened in, I said, "You are right. I am very sorry. Were there times that you wanted to talk to me about something that you were dealing with but did not because you could see I was not doing well?"

They said, "Yes, Daddy. There were times I could tell that you were overwhelmed, so I did not share with you some things I was struggling with because you seemed distracted, and I did not want to bother you."

I teared up. Like most parents, I love our kids and want to do all that I can to be present for them in every way. Our children are a blessing, not a bother. The hard truth that I had failed and burdened our child was something I needed to repent of and ask the family's forgiveness for; I also needed to ask my

Father to help me do a better job as a father. Thankfully our heavenly Father is perfect, and no matter what we need to talk to Him about in prayer, He is never overwhelmed, too busy, or distracted.

As God's children, we've all had times when we should have brought our burdens to Him in prayer but did not. How about you? Have you felt as if your needs were too small, you did not want to be a bother or draw attention to yourself, feared that having needs made you needy, or wondered whether praying for yourself made you selfish?

If Jesus needed to pray, we all do. If Jesus needed to pray for Himself, then you do too.

JESUS' HIGH PRIESTLY PRAYER

Jesus' prayer in John 17 models this life-changing, burden-lifting, hope-giving truth. This prayer is the longest recorded prayer we have from Jesus Christ. It is commonly referred to as Jesus' High Priestly Prayer because He takes the place of the High Priest entering the spiritual holy of holies through prayer, interceding for sinners before the Father. This lengthy prayer does not appear in the synoptic Gospels (Matthew, Mark, and Luke) but is recorded in John's Gospel alone. Had John not included Jesus' prayer, we would be without any record of this great and vital moment in world history.

> If Jesus needed to pray, we all do. If Jesus needed to pray for Himself, then you do too.

Many scholars believe John is "the disciple Jesus loved."[a] So in John 17 we see one of Jesus' most intimate moments in prayer

---

a John 13:23; 19:26; 20:2; 21:7, 20

with His Father related to us honestly by one of Jesus' most intimate friends. It is arguably the richest of Jesus' prayers, and it unfolds with such breadth and depth that Bible students and teachers have been awestruck by its majesty ever since. Marcus Rainsford, the legendary nineteenth-century Irish preacher and friend of the great evangelist D. L. Moody, penned an entire book of more than four hundred pages expounding this great prayer. Scottish pastor and reformer John Knox had it read to him every day as he was dying to prepare himself for eternity. Puritan Bible commentator Matthew Henry says, "The most remarkable prayer followed the most full and consoling discourse ever uttered on earth."[1]

Martin Luther said, "This is truly, beyond measure, a warm and hearty prayer. Jesus opens the depths of His heart, both toward us and His Father, and He pours them all out. It sounds so honest, so simple; it is so deep, so rich, so wide, no one can fathom it."[2] A co-reformer with Luther, lecturing on John 17 as his final talk before his death, said, "There is no voice which has ever been heard, either in heaven or in earth, more exalted, more holy, more fruitful, more sublime, than the prayer offered up by the Son to God Himself."[3] In the nineteenth century, Bishop Ryle said of John 17, "The chapter we have now begun is the most remarkable in the Bible. It stands alone, and there is nothing like it."[4]

To put it simply, John 17 is a big, big deal.

When we are in a loving relationship with someone, the amount of time we spend discussing something with them usually indicates how important the issue is. For example, a couple will spend countless hours discussing their first home purchase and mere minutes picking a restaurant for dinner. How about you? What's the longest prayer you've ever prayed?

Jesus knew that He would be dying very soon. Therein, we are privileged to listen to the inner dialogue of the Trinity as God the Son speaks to God the Father. Of its integral importance and placement, one Bible commentator writes of the prayer:

> Jesus' prayer in chapter 17 is unique to John's Gospel. It is by far the longest prayer of Jesus recorded in any Gospel and comes at a strategic time in Jesus' ministry, sandwiched, as it were, between his final instructions to his closest followers and his passion. Jesus' parting prayer affords us a rare glimpse into his consciousness and perspective on his imminent suffering. Once the prayer is ended, the final events of Jesus' earthly life ensue in rapid succession: the arrest (18:1–11); the Jewish and Roman trials (18:12–19:16); the crucifixion (19:17–37); the burial (19:38–42); the empty tomb and Jesus' resurrection appearances (chs. 20–21). But for one last time, Jesus pauses to take inventory, as it were, of his earthly ministry, giving his final account to the Father and, by praying, expressing his complete dependence on the Father even in this crucial hour.[5]

Jesus' High Priestly Prayer breaks into three sections, which will be explored in this and the following two chapters of this book: Jesus prayed for Himself (vv. 1–5), for Christians (vv. 6–19), and for non-Christians (vv. 20–26).

PRAY FOR YOURSELF

Some people struggle to pray for themselves for a variety of reasons. But remember, Jesus prayed for Himself, and He was perfect. Therefore, it is perfectly good for you to do the same and pray for yourself. If you're struggling with how to do this, here are eight ways you can pray for yourself.

1. Pray to live "kingdom down."

One day, when all is said and done, Jesus Christ will return to earth, bringing the unseen realm of heaven together with the seen realm of earth to answer His prayer, "Your kingdom come, your will be done, on earth as it is in heaven."[b] When all is said and done, eternity will have only two cultures. The culture of hell will be marked by bitterness, isolation, fear, regret, pain, loss, justice, and hopelessness. The culture of heaven will be marked by forgiveness, relationship, faith, thankfulness, blessing, gain, grace, and hope.

Until that day, life on earth has some wonderful days that feel as if heaven has come down and some awful days that feel as if hell has come up. While standing on the earth, between heaven and hell, Jesus "lifted up his eyes to heaven."[c] Before He prayed, Jesus looked up to the Father to remind Himself and us of five faith facts.

- One, this world is not normal. This fractured and frustrating world is flawed by sin. The way things are is not the way things ought to be and not the way they will be eternally. This world has a sin problem. Jesus is the only solution.

- Two, this world is not home. In looking up, Jesus was remembering the heavenly home He had come down from and would be returning to. Jesus was also showing Christians that we too need to keep our eyes fixed on the home that awaits us with Christ.

b Matthew 9:10
c John 17:1

146

- Three, this world is not forever. Roughly one hundred times, English translations of the Bible use phrases such as "endures forever" and "forever and ever" in speaking about God's kingdom of heaven. No nation, culture, organization, or movement can say the same. Therefore, like Jesus, we are to keep our eyes focused on our eternal tomorrow every today.

- Four, we can either look up to God and pray for people in need or look down on people in need. Jesus came to the earth to meet our greatest need—God's forgiveness of sin. In looking up to pray for Himself, and to pray for us, He models for us how to intercede in prayer and do all we can to help others in need.

- Five, this world is where we invite heaven down or pull hell up into our lives through the practical decisions that we make every day. Truth, love, forgiveness, and servanthood are how we invite the Holy Spirit and heaven down into our lives. Lies, hate, bitterness, and selfishness are how we pull unholy spirits and hell up into our lives.

Before we can live kingdom down or heaven down instead of hell up, we need to pray as Jesus did. One reason Jesus endured the hellish horrors of the cross was that He prepared Himself in prayer to push through hell to get to heaven. The same is true of you and me.

2. Pray to deepen your relationship with God.

Our best prayers are often spoken on our worst days. Rather than overeating, drinking, raging, panicking, or self-destructing, Jesus Christ stopped to spend His time and energy praying to get through what He would not get around. In the most difficult season of His life, with crucifixion fast approaching, as countless times before, Jesus began His prayer with the simple word "Father."

Crisis reveals our true selves. In His moment of greatest crisis, Jesus uttered His greatest prayer. In this we see that Jesus rightly regards the darkest and most difficult moments of His life as opportunities rather than obstacles to glorifying God. Jesus' prayer is prayed amid real life, in the moment of His deepest and most urgent need, as our example.

Does God care about you? Yes. He's your Father! Does God listen to you? Yes. He's your Father! Does He want to help you? Yes. Your dad does!

I (Ashley) am reminded that Romans 8:26 says, "For we do not know what to pray for as we ought, but the Spirit himself intercedes for us with groanings too deep for words," which in my life has sometimes looked like feeling so broken that I can only cry or say a few words at a time. "Father" is a good place to start, and I am so thankful that God allows us to come to Him at all times and without pretense. Whether we are praying for ourselves or others, He knows what is going on, and He has felt our pain, so turning to Him is our only hope.

3. Pray to prepare yourself for big changes.

Pain is purposed. It does not lie outside God's will. From Genesis 50:20, where we read that God used for good what Joseph's brothers meant for evil, to Romans 8:28, telling us that "all things" work together for good (and everything in between), we know that pain and suffering and grief are not meaningless for us, nor are they surprises. They are allowed, timed, and purposed by God.

> When Jesus had spoken these words, he lifted up his eyes to heaven, and said, "Father, the hour has come; glorify your Son that the Son may glorify you."
>
> —John 17:1

By referencing this time as "*the* hour," Jesus reveals it is not a surprise. He knew this time was coming beforehand, and He knows it has now come. Likewise, when "the hour" has come for us, we are wise to remember Jesus' words along with Peter's: "Beloved, do not be surprised at the fiery trial when it comes upon you to test you, as though something strange were happening to you."[d]

Jesus does not see this moment of anguish as a glitch in His otherwise trouble-free life and ministry. In fact, "these words" in John 17:1 refer to what Jesus has just been teaching His disciples in the previous chapters. This teaching culminates with Jesus promising them that "in this world you will have trouble," the last verse before His prayer begins.[e]

The hour has arrived, not *an* hour.

Most of us spend our time hoping and even praying moments such as these will not come. In one sense, it is OK to pray nothing bad will happen to you. But if you are alive on this sinful planet, you will sadly suffer. And when some of us suffer, we immediately insist to God that we did not deserve it. We act as if something strange is happening to us.

When these moments come, the best place to go is not

---

d 1 Peter 4:12
e John 16:33, NIV

to fear or fight, but to the Father. And that is exactly what Jesus did.

And as we learned in the Gethsemane prayer, Jesus did not pray to get out of it; He again prays to get *through* it. Winston Churchill is often credited with saying, "If you are going through hell, keep going."[6] Whether he originated the statement or not, it's true. And for Christians, the way to keep going is to keep praying.

Like Jesus, we will all face "the hour" when we have a big decision to make about a big obstacle that inhibits a big opportunity.

After the trying time my family and I (Ashley) went through in ministry, my parents felt called by God to move to Arizona. Most of us kids were not excited about the prospect of living in a desert away from the scenery, family, and friends we were so familiar with. To be honest, I was a bit skeptical, but I trusted that my parents had prayed fervently and heard God. We moved, and after a period of transition, I can see now why God brought us here, and why He wanted me here even though I was old enough to live on my own. I learned to trust my earthly and heavenly fathers, and by seeing my dad's example, I learned that prayer is the best way to make a decision when faced with crisis or confusion since God never loses control of our lives. To Him, everything is history past, not an unknown future. Jesus taught us this first.

4. Pray to glorify God in all you do.

In our homes and cars, we have mirrors. A mirror has one job—to accurately reflect an image so that it can be seen clearly.

We are God's mirror. When Genesis says we were made in God's "image," it means that when God looks at our lives, He should be able to see Himself reflected in our character and conduct. Jesus meant this when He prayed in John 17:1, "Glorify your Son that the Son may glorify you." Paul reflects on all this, saying, "He is the image of the invisible God, the firstborn of all creation."[f]

When we are hurting and life is collapsing, it is not uncommon to feel a bit lost and unsure how to proceed. For the Christian, the will of God is always the same: to glorify Him by reflecting His character no matter what situation we face. This is precisely what Jesus prayed.

Jesus' example is a crucial lesson to learn. We can make our worst decisions on our worst days. Or we can prayerfully determine not to waste our suffering but instead invest it so that our greatest misery leads to our greatest ministry.

I (Ashley) love that my dad always says to "find your crew before your crisis," and to invest in our relationship with God in good times so that when bad times come, we are prepared. If we get into a habit of prayer and time with the Lord when we feel as if things are good or we have time, we will have a better sense of direction and God's will when our world gets shaken or a spiritual attack disorients us. We should also find godly people to help us learn to hear His voice so that they can stand by us in trials, much like Daniel's friends in the Old Testament, who stood by Daniel and pursued God with him, even to the point of literally being put into a furnace. In both the good times and the bad, they were faithful to God and held each other accountable so that God was always glorified.

---

f Colossians 1:15

5. Pray to exercise your authority.

In the physical world, God's people often feel as if they are far more powerless than powerful. In comparison, consider the magnitude of Jesus' prayer, "You have given him authority."[g]

Perhaps the two most important things you and I (Mark) learn in the Bible are 1) who God is and 2) who God says you are. In another book I wrote called *Who Do You Think You Are?* we examine in detail the Christian's identity and who the Bible says you are. More than two hundred times, we are told in Paul's letters that a Christian is "in Christ," "in him," and "in the beloved." This language is not found before Paul and rarely outside of Paul. In comparison, we are called "Christian" only three times in the New Testament.

Positionally we are in Christ. Practically, Christ is in us through the Holy Spirit.

Being in Christ means that just as the Father has given authority to Christ, Christ has given authority to Christians. Ephesians 2:5–6 says, "By grace you have been saved—and [God has] raised us up with him and seated us with him in the heavenly places in Christ Jesus."

When we pray, we are inviting the unseen realm to flood our seen realm, bringing the presence of God to empower our lives. In Scripture, this is exactly what happens when we see the Holy Spirit fall on people. As Jesus headed to the cross, the entire backdrop is spiritual warfare. Leading up to the cross, Satan nearly got Peter to join the demonic rebellion, but Jesus prayed for him: "Simon, Simon, behold, Satan demanded to have you, that he might sift you like wheat, but I have prayed for you."[h]

g John 17:2
h Luke 22:31–32

Judas Iscariot welcomed Satan[i] and conspired with him to betray Jesus and hand Him over to be crucified.

Not only did Satan try to recruit Jesus, Peter, and Judas; Satan will try to recruit you into his rebellion as well. Not only did Jesus prayerfully intercede for Himself to endure suffering and win His spiritual war by exercising His God-given authority, but He also continually prays for you. The Bible says Jesus "always lives to make intercession."[j] The next time you are in a war with the enemy, going through your dark day facing your most frightening fear, pause and prayerfully envision Jesus Christ sitting at the right hand of the Father praying for you to win your war. The same Jesus who interceded for Himself in John 17 is the same "Christ Jesus...at the right hand of God...interceding for us."[k]

One of my (Ashley) favorite portrayals of the meeting of these two realms in the New Testament is of Stephen, who preached the truth of the gospel and was stoned to death for it. As he is dying, he says, "I see the heavens opened, and the Son of Man standing at the right hand of God."[l] Just think about how amazing that would have felt. He had endured spiritual and physical attack at the hands of evil men, yet as his life on earth comes to an end, Jesus stands up from His throne and welcomes him into heaven. I'm sure that seeing Jesus made all his pain feel worthwhile. He had such an eternal view that he even prayed aloud, "Lord, do not hold this sin against them." The Bible then says that he "fell asleep,"[m] just to be raised to live forever with Jesus, who he had fought so valiantly for and

---

i John 13:27
j Hebrews 7:25
k Romans 8:34
l Acts 7:56
m Acts 7:60

loved so fervently, to the point of spending his last few breaths praying to Him. We cling to this hope and authority in prayer.

One of Satan's great lies is telling us we are weak. Over the years, I have prayed with many people who felt they needed prayer in the prayer tent or church instead of praying alone at home. One girl would have nightmares almost every night and would come to the prayer tent in the mornings to be prayed for. I finally explained to her that if she is a Christian, she has authority in Jesus' name to pray for herself and over her bedroom. I was more than happy to pray for her, but I didn't want her to believe that someone "more spiritual" than her in a "spiritual place" would be more effective. She wasn't sure what to pray, so I showed her some examples in the Scriptures, and she immediately felt more empowered knowing that she didn't have to be a victim of Satan's schemes but could boldly pray against them.

6. Pray to live in light of eternity.

Some people are not interested in heaven because it sounds hellish to them. The common cultural caricature of everyone looking like chubby babies in diapers, lounging on white clouds, playing harps, and looking longingly at rainbows and winged unicorns is anything but a good sales pitch. These depictions of heaven that emerged during the Renaissance era of the fifteenth century couldn't be more different from what the Bible tells us.

In His prayer, Jesus reveals that eternal life is a place with a person. "This is eternal life," Jesus says, "that they know you the only true God, and Jesus Christ."[n] Indeed, eternal life is life with God. It is knowing God, being connected to God,

---

n John 17:3

enjoying a relationship with God. Sadly, when eternal life is seen only as a place, the focus on God is lost. The truth is that although heaven is a glorious place, it would be hell if God were not present there.

As I (Mark) travel throughout the year quite a bit, I have had my share of miserable airline flights. I hate to fly—hate it. I always end up squeezed into a narrow seat that would have perfectly fit me when I was under four years of age. The worst is being stuck in the middle seat between two men who make me feel as if I am stuck in a sweaty vice high above the earth.

But when my wife and Ashley's mom, Grace, travels with me, it is an entirely different experience. The arm-rest goes up. She will ask, "Do you want to snuggle?" And of course, I do. We hold hands, we talk, and I enjoy the company of the person I love the most in the world.

Suddenly the flight is fun. And it's all because I am with Grace.

It is a silly illustration, but it works. Heaven would be hell if God were not there with us. Heaven, with all its joys and wonders, is heaven because you get to be with God. When Jesus talks about eternal life, I love that He does not talk about merely where we go but mostly whom we get to be with forever.

I (Ashley) have met so many people, including believers, who don't know anything the Bible says about heaven, and, to be honest, I hadn't studied it in depth until about a year ago when I realized how little I knew. It just didn't seem as important as knowing what to do in this life. But I discovered that the kingdom of God starts on earth, and it is so crucial to get to know the Father here and now because if we are going to be with Him forever, it would be wise to get a glimpse of what that will be like. Then we have both a hope for our own lives and a testimony to share with others so that they don't hold to culture's erroneous views of heaven and, therefore, not accept the gospel as good news.

7. Pray to clarify God's will for you.

When our kids were little, I (Mark) once walked in on one of Ashley's brothers working in the kitchen. The counter was a mess, covered with the oddest assortment of ingredients being combined for what was certain to be far more terrible than tasty. Curious what the plan was, I asked my young son, "What are you doing?" He paused for a moment, thought about it, and replied, "I'm not exactly sure."

We both chuckled.

The truth is, all God's kids find ourselves in the same situation more often than we care to admit. In contrast, at the end of His life, looking back in prayer, Jesus said, "I glorified you on earth, having accomplished the work that you gave me to do."[o]

Jesus articulates the mission of His life on earth, glorifying God by giving eternal life to sinners. With the cross on the horizon, Jesus acknowledged that His death in place of sinners would soon achieve God's glory and their salvation, which together composed the purpose of His mission.

Jesus the Son accomplished what God the Father set out for Him. We can draw two amazing correlations from this. One, Jesus knew what He was supposed to be doing. (Do you know what you are supposed to be doing?) Two, Jesus accomplished what He was supposed to do. (Are you accomplishing what you are supposed to do?)

God invites us to faithfulness, not busyness. Being like Christ does not mean keeping ourselves busy and asking God

---

o John 17:4

to bless our frantic lives. Instead, we need to start with prayer and discover what God's will is for us. Then we can say yes to what we *should* be doing by saying no to lots of other things we *could* be doing.

A wise man who is a loving pastor to our family once noticed that some of our family members, starting with me (Mark), often find ourselves overworked and overwhelmed. Offering us much-needed counsel that echoes the heart of Jesus' prayer, he said, "Don't be moved by need, or opportunity, but only do the will of God."

Those are liberating words. How often have you done something simply because there was a need to meet or opportunity to pursue, but not stopped to pray and confirm that it was God's will for you? This little example from Jesus has big implications and, if heeded, could greatly reduce the historic levels of burnout, anxiety, overwork, and mental health that so many people struggle with.

> *God invites us to faithfulness, not busyness. Being like Christ does not mean keeping ourselves busy and asking God to bless our frantic lives.*

Overcommitting to ministry opportunities has been a struggle my whole life because I (Ashley) feel guilty, as if I am saying no to God if I don't make time for every person and opportunity that comes up. I experienced this problem a lot during my first year of college. I am introverted, which means I need time alone to recharge, but instead of doing this, I would spend far too many hours counseling friends and volunteering in ministries, which led me to feel burned-out. Thankfully some of my mentors helped me set my priorities straight.

These days my husband reminds me that he is my priority

and that if our marriage isn't healthy, we have no business ministering to anyone else. Out of our healthy relationship can come ministry to others, but God doesn't honor or bless our ministry if it is outside His will, no matter how good and helpful it seems. I now constantly pray to ask Him if I have the right heart to serve, one that operates not out of guilt, obligation, or opportunity but out of His will and desire for my life.

8. Pray to experience God's presence.

Jesus tells us that in this life we will suffer, as He did. Therefore, our hope is not to escape suffering but to find God's will in the midst of it. If you cannot get out of tough circumstances, God's presence can get you through them, and that is exactly what Jesus asks the Father for. Jesus closes His prayer for Himself saying, "Father, glorify me in your own presence with the glory that I had with you before the world existed."[p]

These are big words. Jesus reveals Himself to be God by stating that He is eternal (before the world existed) and that He shares the same glory of God the Father with whom He dwelt in eternity past. John begins His Gospel with the words, "In the beginning was the Word, and the Word was with God, and the Word was God. He was with God in the beginning. Through him all things were made; without him nothing was made that has been made."[q]

Like a hose on a bee's nest, Jesus Himself told religious leaders, "Before Abraham was born, I am!"[r] And in numerous other places, Jesus explicitly asserts and implicitly affirms His deity as God. What Jesus is asking for, then, is the revealing of His glory, which was veiled during His earthly ministry. To say

---

p John 17:5
q John 1:1–3, NIV
r John 8:58, NIV

it simply, Jesus is praying for this upside down world to get set right side up, and then He dies and rises to answer His own prayer.

Jesus' prayer at this point is especially insightful theologically because God does not share His glory with anyone else.^s Thus, if

> *You cannot get to God except through Jesus, and you cannot glorify God if you do not glorify Jesus.*

Jesus shares the Father's glory, Jesus is God. One Bible commentator has said:

> The statement in verse 3 is also strikingly similar in form to the central affirmation of Islam, "There is no god but Allah, and Mohammed is his Prophet." Both religions claim to honor the *only true God*, a theme from the Old Testament as well (e.g., Ex 34:6 LXX; Is 37:20), and both speak of the great revealer of God. But they differ radically in what is said of this revealer. Jesus is a prophet—indeed, the revealer of God par excellence. But this verse, in keeping with the whole of this Gospel, says Jesus is far more than just a prophet. For eternal life is not just a knowledge of God as revealed by the Son; it includes a knowledge of the Son himself. Thus he shares in deity, since "the knowledge of God *and a creature* could not be eternal life."...This amazing statement, therefore, affirms both the equality of the Son with the Father and his subordination as son and as the one sent.⁷

This insight adds a lot more weight, then, to Jesus' proclamation that He is the way, the truth, and the life and that no one comes to the Father except through Him. You cannot get to God except through Jesus, and you cannot glorify God if you do not glorify Jesus. While they are distinct persons, they

---

s Isaiah 42:8

share the fullness of deity (as does the Spirit) and therefore share the fullness of glory.

With these words Jesus is looking through His fast-approaching betrayal, arrest, scourging, and crucifixion. He is praying for the vindication of His resurrection that He knows is coming after the deep agony that lay just ahead. In speaking of this return to glory, Jesus refers to the promise of His resurrection; this promise is for victory over Satan, sin, death, hell, and the wrath of God. In His resurrection and ascension back to His heavenly throne over all peoples, times, places, cultures, religions, ideologies, genders, incomes, intellects, and nations, Jesus today has returned to the glory from which He came humbly into history. Jesus prayed for this present reality, laying claim to it as He anticipated the painful prelude of the cross.

The essence of Jesus' prayer thus far is that He would both live and die in such a way as to glorify God the Father. On this theme, one Bible commentator has well said:

> In general, to glorify someone means to hold him or her up for honor and praise. So on one level the Son is asking that his own honor be revealed, namely, that he is one with God; Jesus in turn will glorify the Father as he continues to reveal him as one worthy of all praise and worship. In John, however, glorification also has a more specific meaning: the death of the Son of God. Throughout the Gospel, Jesus has revealed the Father's glory by manifesting his characteristic gracious love. In the death of the Son this same love is revealed most profoundly, for God is love, and love is the laying down of one's life (cf. 1 Jn 4:8, 16; 3:16). Thus, in his death Jesus will reveal his own character and his Father's character to be gracious love.[8]

Jesus models for us the truth that before we can live a life that glorifies God, we need to spend time in heartfelt prayer to know what will glorify God, and then receive the Spirit's power to press forward until God is glorified.

How about you? How should you be praying for yourself? What opportunities has God given you to glorify Him, even by enduring hardship, pain, and injustice? How is your prayer time going with God, and how do you press in to God?

After praying for Himself, Jesus then moves on to pray for the community of His followers, including you, which we will study next.

REFLECTION

1. What does praying for yourself currently look like? What did you learn in this chapter that you can make a part of your prayer life?

2. Do you turn to prayer when life gets dark and uncertain? How do you try to discern God's will and get through it?

3. Looking back, how do you now see God in both the highs and lows of your life?

4. What does heaven have to do with prayer?

5. Do you think about glorifying God in your daily life? How did Jesus glorify God?

Chapter 8

PRAY FOR CHRISTIANS

The Lord's High Priestly Prayer, Part 2

I have manifested your name to the people whom you gave me out of the world. Yours they were, and you gave them to me, and they have kept your word. Now they know that everything that you have given me is from you. For I have given them the words that you gave me, and they have received them and have come to know in truth that I came from you; and they have believed that you sent me. I am praying for them. I am not praying for the world but for those whom you have given me, for they are yours. All mine are yours, and yours are mine, and I am glorified in them. And I am no longer in the world, but they are in the world, and I am coming to you. Holy Father, keep them in your name, which you have given me, that they may be one, even as we are one. While I was with them, I kept them in your name, which you have given me. I have guarded them, and not one of them has been lost except the son of destruction, that the Scripture might be fulfilled. But now I am coming to you, and these things I speak in the world, that they may have my joy fulfilled in themselves. I have given them your word, and the world has hated them because they are not of the world, just as I am not of the world. I do not ask that you take them out of the world, but that you keep them from the evil one. They are not of the world, just as I am not of the world. Sanctify them in the truth; your word is truth. As you sent me into the world, so I have sent them into the world. And for their sake I consecrate myself, that they also may be sanctified in truth.
—JOHN 17:6–19

EVERY AIRLINE FLIGHT starts with the sharing of the same basic information. We are told that to remain healthy and helpful, should the need arise, we should first put the oxygen mask on ourselves, then help those closest to us, and finally help others. The logic makes sense. Unless you are doing well, along with the people closest to you, you cannot be of much help to others.

Life is a lot like a flight. There's bound to be turbulence now and then, and prayer is our way of getting the proverbial mask on and inviting the Holy Spirit to do for our soul what oxygen does for our body. For this reason Jesus models praying for oneself, then for fellow Christians, and finally for non-Christians.

After praying for Himself, Jesus proceeds to pray for His followers, who would come to believe in Him as God and would subsequently bring the good news of His person and work to the world.

Jesus refers to these Christians as people who accept that He was sent by God the Father into history to reveal His "name." This shorthand way of describing someone's character, attributes, and essence reminds me of old cop movies where the officer demands that the criminal stop "in the name of the law," meaning by order of the full authority of the entire legal system. This little prayer gives us big insight into Jesus' heart and mind on His darkest days.

JESUS DOES NOT PRAY FOR THE WORLD

If someone came up to you and asked you to pray that God would help them commit murder or adultery, you would not pray for them. Why? Because what they were doing was completely opposed to the will, way, and Word of God, therefore, it's nothing to ask God to bless. When Jesus says, "I do not pray for the world,"[a] this is the gist of what He means.

This statement is understandably confusing to many because the Greek word translated "world" is used in at least seven senses throughout the New Testament. Sometimes it means the entire creation, sometimes the inhabited world, sometimes people, sometimes the fallen system of attitudes and values that run counter to God's design, and sometimes various shades of each of those things. Context is always key.

What these particular words *do not* mean is that Jesus does not love everyone. When He says He is not praying for the world, it does not mean He discriminates against certain types of humanity. Jesus loves people of all races and cultures, and the great heavenly worship song tells us that Jesus' blood purchases men "from every tribe and language and people and nation."[b]

When Jesus says, "I do not pray for the world," He is referring to the system of thinking, speaking, and acting in rebellion to God, in allegiance to Satan, and at war against the kingdom of heaven. Echoing Jesus, this is the "world" the apostle Paul most often warns against in his letters. Jesus does not pray for the world to be sanctified, joyful, sent, or glorified because it is against Him and cannot be changed until it submits to Him.

Everything that God creates, Satan counterfeits. The world is the counterfeit of the kingdom of God, run by demons who are the counterfeit of angels. They tell lies, which is the counterfeit of truth, and encourage rebellion, which is the counterfeit of holiness. When Jesus came, He did not come to save demons but only people. Unlike people, there is no possibility

---

a John 17:9, NKJV
b Revelation 5:9

of salvation for demonic powers or redemption of their works in the world. Jesus does not pray for the demonic spirits at work behind the world system forming culture, running economies, driving education, dominating politics, and creating entertainment, because there is no hope for them.

This example of Jesus cannot be overlooked. Not only does He pray for Christians in the church as the outpost of the kingdom, but He also prays against demonic powers and the world, which is at war against Christians and the kingdom. Too often Christians learn to pray defensively only after they have suffered a spiritual attack. Jesus models offensive prayers where we pray against every and any power and principality that might come against the holiness of Christians and the honor of Christ.

JESUS PRAYS FOR OUR KEEPING

Over the years, Grace and I (Mark) have known a lot of families where either the husband or wife decides, for whatever reason, that they are not going to remain devoted to the relationship. Sometimes this includes a separation where they move out of the house for a season to decide what their long-term plan is.

Whenever this happens, there ultimately cannot be a healthy, lengthy future unless they both decide to be devoted to working on the relationship. However, for a season the relationship can survive with the hope of being saved if at least one person remains faithfully devoted to the other.

In our relationship with God, the wonderful news is that "if we are faithless, he remains faithful."[c] Our God is rock steady in His love, devotion, and character. When we wander, He waits for us to return and never closes His heart toward us as

---

c 2 Timothy 2:13

Christians. Our Father loves us and is completely committed to "keeping" us.

We maintain our relationship with God because our God keeps us.

Our relationship with God is not maintained because we have it all together, walk faithfully, keep our chin up, or never trip over our own feet. We do persevere; we do work out our salvation as Philippians 2:12 tells us. But the next verse reminds us that it is God who works in us. Salvation is a work God does in us, and our obedience is a work God does through us, as the fruit of Christ's perfect life grows in us in the power of the Holy Spirit. God is a good Father who promises to keep us and has promised never to leave us or forsake us.[d] Once again, so much of our prayer life and emotional health comes down to knowing and trusting the Father heart of God.

One of the blessings God has given our family is the opportunity to travel. When I (Ashley) was in middle school and my siblings were much younger, we went to Israel and Turkey. At one time we were staying in a hotel and decided to take the elevator down to get something to eat. We all got in but realized we had left something in the room, so we got out to grab it—all of us minus my six-year-old sister, who didn't notice we had all gotten off the elevator. She waved to us as the doors closed and she began her lonely ride to an unknown floor. My parents, of course, panicked and quickly ran through the options, ultimately deciding that my dad would take the stairs and check every floor of the hotel in case she got off, while my mom would go down to the lobby with the rest of us to see whether she ended up there. A minute after we arrived, Alexie

---

d Hebrews 13:5

ended up in the lobby with the rest of us, perfectly safe and sound.

Thankfully my parents didn't wait for Alexie to find us, as she was lost and helpless and very young. They came up with a plan that kept the other four of us safe but allowed them to search for Alexie and cover the most ground as quickly as possible. She had technically gotten herself in trouble, but now it was my parents' responsibility to get her out. Throughout all our travels, they watched over and kept us safe, sometimes having to step in if we wandered.

God is the same way. Some of His children wander more than others, but we are all kept by the same hand and watchful eye. We are not lost, because He keeps us found.

Christians often ask whether someone can lose their salvation. I (Mark) believe that while the answer is no, the question is flawed. The real question is, Will the Father disown His child? To stress this point, Jesus prays aloud so others can overhear and learn, "Not one of them has been lost."[e]

Not long after this prayer, a disciple of Jesus would completely disown and destroy Christ. This series of events leads to confusion for some regarding the role of Judas Iscariot, who betrayed Jesus before hanging himself.

In Judas we tragically learn that you cannot lose your salvation, but you can fake it. Christianity is not mere lip service but a lifestyle based on a love for Jesus above all else. Judas faked faith with mere lip service. Jesus said of Judas, "One of you is a devil."[f] Stealing money from Jesus' ministry the entire

---

e John 17:12
f John 6:70

time they were together, "he was a thief."[g] And in a counterfeit sign of being Spirit-filled, "Satan entered into him."[h]

Tragically Judas serves as a painful reminder that living three years with Jesus, witnessing His miracles, hearing His teaching, and seeing His life are not enough to save someone unless they are accompanied by faith in and love for Jesus as God. Though God foreknew what Judas would do, Judas was no victim because he freely chose evil. Judas' fake faith was prophesied well in advance, as God, who rules the future, revealed it in advance so that we could trust God to keep us and not be frightened by the fate of Judas.

David prophesied roughly a thousand years in advance that Jesus would be betrayed by a friend, "Even my close friend in whom I trusted, who ate my bread, has lifted his heel against me."[i] This prophecy was fulfilled when "[Judas] came up to Jesus at once and said, 'Greetings, Rabbi!' And he kissed him. Jesus said to him, 'Friend, do what you came to do.'"[j]

Zechariah prophesied five hundred years in advance that Jesus' betraying friend would be paid thirty pieces of silver for handing Him over to the authorities and that the payment would be thrown in the temple in disgust before the year AD 70, when it was destroyed.[k] This prophetic betrayal occurs when "one of the twelve, whose name was Judas Iscariot, went to the chief priests and said, 'What will you give me if I deliver him over to you?' And they paid him thirty pieces of silver," which was then tossed "into the temple."[l]

If you have a painful history with a ministry leader who

---

g John 12:6
h John 13:27
i Psalm 41:9
j Matthew 26:49–50
k Zechariah 11:12–13
l Matthew 26:14–15; 27:5–7

completely abandoned the faith, the story of Judas is meant to provide clarity for you. If you have a loved one who has strayed from the Lord but you believe they are genuinely saved, the story of the prodigal son is meant to provide comfort for you. The prodigal was still a son even when he was astray for a season, whereas Judas never was a son of God but rather a "son of destruction."[m]

JESUS PRAYS FOR GODLY UNITY
OVER DEMONIC DIVISION

There are many reasons that our first instinct is often to be independent, rebellious, and not part of a group under authority. First, we are all children of Adam. Our sinful nature is like a gravitational force that pulls us toward pride and autonomy so that we think we are better and wiser than we are and need God and others less than we do.

Second, Christian Protestantism was birthed in protest. We are Reformed and Protestant by biblical conviction. Still, there is sadly a downside to our form of faith, as we seem to keep up the spirit of protesting in every generation, which makes unity under authority a near impossibility.

Third, if you live in our nation, we were founded on the principle of independence and celebrate it every year on July 4 by eating too much and blowing things up in the name of freedom. Again, we love our country and appreciate its freedoms, but the same ethos that caused us to break from external authority, if not checked, can cause us to break apart all together into total anarchy.

Fourth, most everyone alive today was born on the other side of the countercultural rebellion of the 1960s and 1970s.

---

m John 17:12

The new trinity was sex, drugs, and rock and roll as families were divided generationally. It is now wrongly and dangerously assumed that every generation will rebel against the one before it as a rite of passage.

Now, consider how crucial this portion of Jesus' prayer is: "That they may be one, even as we are one."[n] Jesus speaks of true Christians being able to live together as "one" just as the Trinitarian community of God the Father, Son, and Spirit live together as "one." This unity should begin in marriage between a husband and wife whom God made to be "one." Sadly, Christian unity is constantly undermined by sins within us and forces outside us, which means unity requires a continuous effort.

God works through unity, and Satan works through division. There was no division until Satan chose to become independent, rebel, and cause division by recruiting angels to become demons in a coup attempt. On earth, Satan continues to recruit human beings to join the demons in their division against God. For the Christian, there simply cannot be any health or holiness without unity, and division is the doorway to the demonic.

Unity does not mean uniformity. Like any family, God's family has a lot of diversity. Division does not mean distinction. Different Christians can have different methods for how they live their lives while maintaining unity on the principles behind them. For the Christian, unity begins by valuing our relationship with God and others above our personal and pet issues. Issues are secondary; relationships are primary. The only way we should divide with a professing Christian is if they divide from God over a closehanded, primary issue (for

---

n John 17:11

example, the Bible being God's Word, Jesus being the only way to salvation, and so on). If our disagreement is on an open-handed, secondary issue, we need to pray for them, pray with them, and build our relationship so that it is strong enough not to be broken by the issue we are disagreeing on. (I'll discuss more about closehanded and openhanded issues in chapter 9.)

In the church family, this unity is to be theological (what we believe), relational (how we love), missional (what we do), and organizational (how we coexist). The church is a big family, and as with any big family, unity has to be the priority and comes at a cost.

> Unity begins by valuing our relationship with God and others above our personal and pet issues.

There is a reason Jesus called twelve guys and told them to follow Him. There is a reason Paul refers to the church as a body. It is ridiculous to think an eyeball can be of any use apart from its place in a head, attached to a neck, attached to a torso, attached to a body. You are not meant to live the Christian life alone. Your personal relationship with Jesus includes other persons.

Jesus knew we would need to get along once He left, which is why He prayed for us. Similar to a dad headed out of town for a trip, He reminds the kids to love and look out for one another when He says to the Father, "Now I am coming to you."o

The disciples would eventually experience Jesus' ascension as doubly bittersweet. In the joy of seeing Him resurrected, they would be saddened by His departure to be with the Father. But in the sadness of His departure, they would have

---

o John 17:13

the joy of receiving the gift of the Holy Spirit and His comforting presence.

Jesus' going to the Father is important for us because He promised that where He was going we would also be. And He promised that He was going there to prepare a place for us. This promise is how incredibly good our Savior and brother Jesus is to us: He not only goes before us into death and the grave to be our substitute; He goes before us into heaven to get the place ready for our eternal home. Jesus' gracious work is the source of deepest joy.

Prayer truly is the unifying force of believers, as it invites the kingdom down instead of allowing earthly culture to divide us. As I've mentioned, in college I (Ashley) hosted a monthly united prayer gathering that invited different Christian ministries to join together in prayer for our campus since in the end we all had the same goal to see souls won for Jesus. At such a large university, it was encouraging to see God using each ministry to reach a specific group of students, ultimately coming together to see the whole campus reached by each ministry fulfilling God's specific will. There was no need for competition among ministries when we all submitted to God's will, and the same can be true for staff at a church, churches within a city, and believers in general.

> You are not meant to live the Christian life alone. Your personal relationship with Jesus includes other persons.

JESUS PRAYS FOR OUR JOY

Jesus' next words in this portion of the prayer are about joy: "That they may have my joy."[p] Simply put, the life of a Christian, like the life of Jesus, is not always marked by great comfort, wealth, health, ease, or simplicity. Nevertheless, it is filled with the presence of God and the purpose of God so that all we have, do, and endure can and will be used to glorify God and benefit others as it was with Jesus when He went to the cross.

The Christian life is one of joy—not the kind of joy that most people seek, but the kind of joy Jesus had. Do not waste a single second of your life—not even the bad parts or the dark parts. Do not put your life on autopilot when the going gets rough. Jesus is praying in John 17 about a good life, not an *easy* life. There is a *big* difference!

The one who did not have hope, who lost hope, was Judas. Jesus and Judas are the two examples of how to live one's life. Jesus hung from a tree for the glory of God and joy of the world, a precursor to reigning in glory forever. Judas hung from a tree in a noose of his own making after gaining some money but losing his soul.

Jesus reflects a God-honoring, God-glorifying life, not a comfortable life. In fact, Jesus promises trouble.

As He heads to the cross to suffer, Jesus prays for another source of joy for us—it is the joy of knowing this world is not our home. Despite all the pain and suffering we might endure here, what an encouragement it can be to know that this is not our forever home! This world is a place where we love and serve people and—yes—endure, but we are essentially "just passing through."

Our joy amid our broken and fallen world is in knowing

---

p John 17:13

who Jesus is, what He has done in us, and the future He has planned for us. Preceding this prayer, Jesus teaches in John 16 that He will die for our sins, rise for our salvation, and send the Holy Spirit to renew, indwell, empower, and transform us so that we can participate with God in seeking lost people caught in the trap of this world. For the Christian, heaven does not begin the day you die but rather the day you start living for Jesus! Jesus' final words in John that precede His High Priestly Prayer are "In the world you will have tribulation. But take heart; I have overcome the world."[q]

Our joy is not found, then, by our current state in the world (that place of sin and rebellion against God) but rather by the presence and power of God in us *even while we are in the world.* For this we rejoice because for the Christian, this world is as close to hell as we will ever get and we are almost home to heaven.

What will you do with the darkness? Don't waste it. Lean in to God through it. "Let us look only to Jesus, the One who began our faith and who makes it perfect. He suffered death on the cross. But he accepted the shame as if it were nothing because of the joy that God put before him. And now he is sitting at the right side of God's throne."[r]

> Our joy amid our broken and fallen world is in knowing who Jesus is, what He has done in us, and the future He has planned for us.

---

q John 16:33
r Hebrews 12:2, NCV

JESUS PRAYS FOR OUR PROTECTION

There are billions of Christians alive on the earth today, in addition to those from the past and future. In John 17, Jesus was praying for all of us. He was praying for you, your church, your pastor, your small group, and your family members.

If you knew it was your last hour, what would you pray? Who would you pray for? In Jesus' prayer, as you would expect, He does pray for Himself (as we saw in the previous chapter), but He spends most of His prayer interceding for us and praying for our protection.

We are born sinners by nature and by choice, and this world we live in is the place where sin is made available and attractive. Think of the world as a bunch of hooks with different bait hung on each one: sex, money, status, beauty, power, fame, comfort, food, religion, drug abuse, and so on. These hooks are set by Satan, whose mission it is to tempt us with this bait. And we are swimming along, conned by our sinful appetites, checking out all the lures the world has to offer. And we think that when we bite the right one, we will find joy. But we never do.

We live in a nation founded on the pursuit of happiness. Everyone is pursuing joy, but nobody is finding it. That is because they are pursuing joy out in the world. But our joy cannot be found in the world. It can only be fulfilled in us by God.

Jesus must do something in us that makes joy a gift to us. This gift of joy is the gift of the Holy Spirit, which Jesus promised just before this prayer[s] and which Jesus is anticipating in this prayer as the comfort coming after His death, resurrection, and ascension.

---

s John 16:5–16

Before Jesus we all seek our joy in the world. Some of our pursuits are not bad things but good things in the wrong place. Making good things into ultimate things changes them to bad things. If anyone or anything takes God's place as our highest priority or deepest passion, things have gone bad because a good thing has displaced God. The center of our universe, apart from a miracle, is self, and the world is to fulfill *me*, please *me*, serve *me*, satisfy *me*. When Jesus saves us and the Holy Spirit begins to reside in us, our relationship with the world changes. The world suddenly becomes the place where we give rather than take.

The truth is, the closer you get to Jesus, the sadder the world becomes. One thing people who don't know Jesus don't understand is that the Holy Spirit changes our desires. The Christian does not fight against temptation, read the Bible, pray, get connected to a church, give a percentage of their income back to the Lord, or volunteer in a ministry because they have to even though they hate it. No, the Christian gets to do what they want to do because God has changed their desires. For the Christian, when we obey God and live as He created us to, we experience a deep and profound joy that someone who does not have the Spirit cannot understand in the same way that a blindfolded person cannot enjoy a sunset.

The world is marked with the life-damaging effects of sin and pain and death. One of the devil's most powerful lies is telling us joy is out there in the world. When you become a Christian, what was tempting in the world now strikes you as tragic. What you used to enjoy you are now ashamed of. What you used to brag about you now mourn. What you used to attend parades for you now have funerals for. When God changed you, your relationship with the world changed, and He doesn't want it to change back.

Jesus Prays for Our Mission

If the world is not our home, the obvious question is, Why are we here? The answer is to be missionaries.

The question before us is not, Are we missionaries? The real question is, Are we good missionaries or bad ones?

Like any relationship, the way strangers become friends is when a mutual friend introduces them. This principle is the heart of missional living—introducing people in the world who don't know God to the God who made them and loves them.

"Missions" is a calling for all Christians since we all have our part to play in God's mission. The prevailing thought used to be that the church sends missionaries across the water to people who don't know God. But we cross paths with people who don't know God every day.

Jesus helps us figure out how to be good missionaries with His words on being *in* the world but not *of* it. Every area of the world needs missionaries, and all Christians need to be missionaries. Jesus loves the lost people who cross our paths, and He sent us to take His love to them.

For this reason, every Christian must love people, serve people, and engage people. It is why every Christian must learn about local cultures and seek to contextualize the gospel in those cultures. Effective missionaries to China learn the language, learn the customs, engage in the cultural narratives, and contextualize the gospel for the understanding of the Chinese people. In the same way, part of our mission in all corners of the world and its contexts means listening to people, empathizing, reading the literature, pounding the cultural pavement, even understanding the entertainment. We want to understand people because we are then best able to help them. We also learn from the example of Jesus' own life as a missionary. We see in the Gospels that Jesus doesn't interact with people on a superficial level. He *knows* the people—tax collectors and sinners, Samaritans and Romans, the community of His disciples from all walks of life, and even the religious Pharisees and the political Sadducees. Jesus lives among them and invests in relationships with them. He goes to their events and participates in their culture. He accepts invitations to weddings and parties. He enters other cultures (as in Samaria). Over and over, we see Jesus working hard to serve as the best missionary ever.

With the sacrifice of the cross on the horizon, Jesus prays, "Father, just as you sent me, I am sending them."[t] Just as God has sent Jesus to a time and place, He has sent you to a time and place. And just as God sent Jesus to sacrifice for the love of the world, you are called to take up your cross, deny yourself, and love people in the world. Just as Jesus was a missionary, we are to be missionaries. And if God should move you to another place, you are to be a missionary there as well.

JESUS PRAYS AGAINST REBELLION

We must take care, however, in all our serving, investing, interacting, and contextualizing that we do not blend in to the point of inconsequence. Think of it as a boat on the water. The boat is supposed to be in the water; the water is not supposed to be in the boat. Otherwise the boat sinks under the water. A Christian in this world is supposed to be part of Jesus' rescue mission, rowing through this world, finding lost people adrift

---

t John 17:18

at sea, and helping pull them into the boat with us while not taking in water and sinking the boat.

Being on a mission for Jesus starts with being sanctified like God and sent by God. Jesus declares that He was sanctified from the world even though He was sent into it.[u] Jesus is *not* saying that He was growing in holiness and diminishing in sin; no, He was and is perfectly holy and altogether without sin. Rather, Jesus is saying He was set apart for the purposes of God and sent by God the Father into the world. One Bible commentator explains Jesus' words in this way:

> ("I sanctify/consecrate myself") is to be understood as an act of committing himself to the holy will of the Father and in dedicating himself to Calvary...In this sense to consecrate himself meant to be set aside for God's special purpose. Consecration is also identified in the Torah with sacrifice (Deut 15:19), a sacrifice that usually implied the death of the offering. In consecrating himself, Jesus modeled for his disciples what is meant to be both alien from the world and yet committed to a mission in and to the world, even to the point of death.[1]

Sanctified in this context means "set apart." When my husband and I (Ashley) were creating our wedding registry, we had some laughs deciding what kitchen items to add. As a bachelor living alone, he was a newbie at choosing things like dinnerware and to my surprise did not share my strong opinions about what dishes are used for what purposes. We decided on a set that had soup bowls, and I chose some additional cereal bowls as well to complement it. He was confused about why we needed more than one set of bowls and said that as long as he had something to eat cereal out of, he didn't care whether it

---

u John 17:19

was specifically a "cereal bowl," so I explained that soup bowls are for soup but cereal bowls are for cereal. There are different shapes for different purposes. We received and have used both sets of bowls, but I still laugh when I see him using one for something other than its intended purpose.

Being sanctified for mission means living lives of holiness and being distinct in our conduct and in our faithfulness to show people in the world what kingdom life looks like with Jesus. If we are sanctified that way, we will go into the world on a mission while not becoming "of the world." The goal is to convert sinners to Christ, not Christians to sin. Christians have a different type of involvement with sex, money, alcohol, community, and other things the world abuses. This sort of living is countercultural living, and the gospel of the kingdom creates a countercultural community of missionaries.

For instance, Jesus is a friend to single women, but He does not lust, fornicate, or commit adultery. Jesus goes to parties, but He does not get drunk or high or dance with a lampshade on His head.

Jesus' example teaches us that contrary to the Pharisees of His day and the religious eggheads of today, we should enjoy friendships with non-Christians and enjoy the culture and the city. We should intentionally love our communities and want what is best for them, but we engage in all this missionary activity without succumbing to the bait Satan sets out for us in the world. We are free to connect as missionaries do. We go into the world not merely to be entertained but to be educated.

The sort of sanctification that Jesus urges here is imperative. Before Jesus began His earthly ministry, the Spirit led Him into the desert to be tempted by the devil. The devil tempted Jesus to abuse pleasure, exploit His position, and embrace ambition. The same temptations await us every day.

In one of the most power-packed missional verses in all Scripture, Jesus prayerfully warned Christians that they have two purposes in the world: to be sanctified (or set apart by God for His purposes) and sent into the world. He also warned them of two pitfalls in the world, two enemies of being a good missionary: religion (legalism) and rebellion (liberalism).

JESUS PRAYS AGAINST RELIGION

When Jesus prayed for you and the rest of us, "Do not...take them out of the world,"[v] He prayed against religion. A misunderstanding of sin and holiness wrongly thinks that if we don't want to be tainted, we had better disengage from the world. So we separate ourselves and create holiness codes not found in the Bible to ensure distance from lost people is maintained. This mentality results in the creation of a Christian bunker to hide in.

You probably know Christians like this. Maybe you are one. This disengaged kind of living gets it only half right. It takes the command "Be holy" very seriously, but it further extrapolates it into all kinds of religious rules, which is religious sin and not holiness. Suddenly we have taken something the Bible says and turned it into lots of things the Bible doesn't say: real Christians don't watch movies; real Christians don't drink or listen to "secular"

> A misunderstanding of sin and holiness wrongly thinks that if we don't want to be tainted, we had better disengage from the world.

---

v John 17:15

music; real Christians don't play card games; real Christians don't fraternize with lost people. Suddenly we've burned the bridge from the kingdom to the world and no longer have access to the lost people we are called to reach for Christ.

Jesus' efforts were intended not to capitulate to rebellion in the world but rather to call the world to repentance. Subsequently, those people in the world who remain unrepentant hated Jesus in His day and continue to hate Him in our day. They hated Him because He stood against the world, even though He was only doing so out of love for people, inviting them to a better way of life through Him. They did not hate Him because He was removed from them, creating a subculture with minimal interaction with the wider culture. No, Jesus lived a holy life amid unholy people, and He calls us to do the same so that they see an alternative to the only way of life they have ever known.

Speaking to all Christians who would come to believe in Him, Jesus frankly told us that we should not be surprised when the world hates us too, as we live as missionaries in the world. This hatred can take any number of forms, such as being mocked, gossiped about, criticized, persecuted, fired, hated, slandered, sued, and even in some cases, martyred. Again, every Christian is—like Jesus—a missionary sent by God into the world to the time and place God has appointed for them and is to be sanctified or set apart for God's purposes. The more effective we are at this calling, the more the world will hate us.

A Bible commentator has said of this section of Jesus' prayer:

> This verse [John 17:18] confirms the fact that the main focus of this section of the prayer is on the preparation of the disciples for mission. The disciples, like Jesus, would experience

the sense of being aliens in the hostile world (17:14), but this prayer does not advocate abandoning the world to the devil. Quite the opposite is true because just as it has been repeatedly said throughout this Gospel that the Father sent Jesus into the world, so it is here clearly asserted that Jesus has sent his followers into the world. The Greek verb *apostellein* occurring twice carries the idea of being sent for a purpose or being sent on a mission. The English word "apostle" is obviously derived from this Greek word family, and apostleship must accordingly be understood not so much as a status but as a purposeful calling to a mission by Jesus.[2]

Jesus prays against the other pitfall facing missional living: rebellion and liberalism. "Keep them from the evil one,"[w] He asks the Father.

Rebellious Christians think people are not that bad and that Satan and his demons are not really at work. They move into cities and learn what is going on in the cultures, and they become politically and socially active, and they genuinely want to help people. Still, through it all, they end up compromising their sanctification. In rebellion and liberalism, the church is a mirror of the world. Do you think homosexuality is OK? Hey, so do we! Do you think fornication is OK? Hey, so do we! Do you think God made a mistake with someone's gender so they can choose to remake their sex? Hey, so do we! Do you think everyone goes to heaven in the end? Hey, so do we!

> Jesus lived a holy life amid unholy people, and He calls us to do the same so that they see an alternative to the only way of life they have ever known.

---

w John 17:15

Rebellion and theological liberalism overemphasize being sent into the world to the degree that it forgets that we are supposed to be sanctified and set apart for God, distinct from the world by living in a way that is holy and pleasing to God. In other words, we can become so concerned about being missionaries connecting with the culture that we forget to be faithful Christians connecting to God. While religion and legalism lead to sectarianism and isolationism, the sinful forgetfulness of rebellion and liberalism inevitably leads to syncretism. *Syncretism* is where people so love, understand, sympathize with, and even wrongly accommodate the world that they are no longer distinct from the world and hated by it as Jesus expects. Rather than being a mirror that reflects the kingdom of God to the world, they are a mirror reflecting the world to itself.

These are the two pitfalls Jesus prays against: religion and rebellion. These are the age-old pendulum swings of legalism, which does not go far enough into the world, and liberalism, which goes too far into the world. Both views have aspects of truth in them, but both views are wrong. We are to be sanctified *and* sent.

Jesus reveals this problem in the story of the prodigal son. The older brother is the religious one with lots of legalisms, including not entering the home of his sinful brother. The younger brother is the rebellious one with lots of liberal behavior as he breaks the hearts of both his earthly father and heavenly Father.

The third way between religion and rebellion is the path blazed by Jesus Himself that He prayed we would follow. Stay holy and live sent. Read and believe all the verses, not just the ones you like. We are not going to be *of* the world because

Jesus wasn't and asked that we not be, but we are going to be *in* the world because Jesus was and said that we too should be.

No, it is not easy. But it is joyful. It is the way of Jesus.

How do we navigate this path, this third way? Jesus asks the Father to sanctify us by the truth. What is the truth? His Word is truth.[x] That is why we are Bible-believing, Bible-trusting, Bible-reading Christians. If you want a word *from* God, you need to open the Word *of* God. If you want to find the way to walk the tightrope between religion and rebellion, you have to open your heart to the Spirit and mind to the Bible so that you can walk with Jesus by following in His footsteps. Relationship with Jesus is the only way to avoid religion on the right and rebellion on the left.

The order of Jesus' prayer is, of course, our perfect example. First, pray for yourself to be close to God and aligned with His will. Second, pray for yourself and fellow Christians to work together in unity to see people saved by Jesus. Our personal holiness and the character of our Christian families and church families are not the end goal but rather a means to the end goal, which is being sent by God on a mission in the world as Jesus was to see people meet Jesus. Someone did this for us, and in response, we are blessed to do the same for someone else as part of God's divine pay-it-forward plan.

> If you want a word from God, you need to open the Word of God.

JESUS STILL PRAYS FOR YOU

It is amazing to consider that on one of Jesus' darkest and most difficult days, He stopped to pray for you and the rest of

---

x John 17:17

us who are Christians. Even more amazing, Jesus continues to pray for us and is doing so right now. Jesus "is able to save to the uttermost those who draw near to God through him, since he always lives to make intercession for them," because, "Christ Jesus is the one who died—more than that, who was raised—who is at the right hand of God, who indeed is interceding for us."[y]

Right now Jesus is aware of what you are going through, including the hopes you have, burdens you bear, and fears you face. Right now Jesus is talking to the Father and Spirit, along with angels and other divine beings, about you as He intercedes for you. The High Priestly Prayer continues every moment of every day and should be an incredible encouragement that you are loved and prayed for and someone is staying up all night concerned for you and interceding for you!

REFLECTION

1. Do you currently pray for Christians? How can you improve in this practice?

2. Are you living in a way that is unified with fellow believers? How?

3. Are you a good missionary? What can you learn from Jesus about living on mission wherever God has put you?

4. How do you find joy in suffering?

5. Are you living in the world or of it?

---

y Hebrews 7:25; Romans 8:34

Chapter 9

PRAY FOR NON-CHRISTIANS

The Lord's High Priestly Prayer, Part 3

*I do not ask for these only, but also for those who will believe in me
through their word, that they may all be one, just as you, Father,
are in me, and I in you, that they also may be in us, so that the
world may believe that you have sent me. The glory that you have
given me I have given to them, that they may be one even as we are
one, I in them and you in me, that they may become perfectly one,
so that the world may know that you sent me and loved them even
as you loved me. Father, I desire that they also, whom you have
given me, may be with me where I am, to see my glory that you
have given me because you loved me before the foundation of the
world. O righteous Father, even though the world does not know you,
I know you, and these know that you have sent me. I made known
to them your name, and I will continue to make it known, that the
love with which you have loved me may be in them, and I in them.*
—JOHN 17:20–26

A S A TEENAGE boy, I (Mark) grew up knowing a few
things about Jesus, but not knowing Jesus. In our not-
so-great public high school, my favorite teacher was a
Christian. We all knew this because he kept a large, well-worn
leather-bound Bible on his desk for everyone to see. Whenever

there was a break, including lunch, he could be found sitting alone at his desk with his Bible open, reading. He always dressed neatly in a suit, had his white hair combed perfectly, and carried himself as a dignified gentleman.

To be honest, he was one of the toughest teachers in the school when it came to classwork. He was also one of the tenderest teachers when it came to caring for his students. Almost anytime the students were asked to vote for one faculty member to speak at an assembly or graduation, he was chosen. Despite the fact that if you took his class, your grade point average would likely go down a bit, his classes were always full because students learned and were loved.

In college I became a Christian and was very thankful for the testimony of my former teacher. It was rumored that he was a volunteer pastor at his church, preaching some of the time. Since God had called me to be a pastor, I decided to drop by my old school one day when I was home from college on break. I found him sitting at his desk, reading his Bible as usual. Since he was alone, I hoped we'd have a few minutes to chat. He warmly greeted me, we sat down, and I told him that I had become a Christian and was studying the Bible to become a pastor. This sturdy former military man started weeping tears of joy, leaped out of his chair, came around the desk, and gave me a huge hug.

He told me that he had been praying for me for years, asking God to bring me into a relationship with Jesus Christ. He further explained that although he was not supposed to evangelize kids due to school district policy, he felt called to teach so that he could pray for students and leave his Bible in plain view so that if they wanted to ask questions about God or be prayed for they knew where to come. He then told me the stories of numerous other students I knew who had also become Christians in recent years.

Before I left, I asked him if he could lay hands and pray over me since he was a pastor and I was called to become a pastor. He laughed and said, "I have been praying for you for years, and I will pray for you today, and I will keep praying for you!" He prayed and hugged me, and I exited his office filled with encouragement. I was shocked that he took the time to pray for me and many others over the years. To this day, every time I read the final section of Jesus' prayer in John 17, where the rabbi/teacher prays for non-Christians to be saved, I think of my old teacher praying for me and many others to become Christians.

JESUS PRAYS FOR NON-CHRISTIANS

Amazingly, anyone who has become a Christian had Jesus pray for them to have their sins forgiven. The timing of this prayer is incredible.

In the Gospel of John, half of the entire Gospel is devoted to the final week leading up to Jesus' death. As He heads to the cross to pay the penalty for our sin, Jesus is praying that we would come to believe in Him for salvation.

When Jesus prayed, "I do not ask for these only, but also for those who will believe in me through their word,"[a] He was praying for you. It is a bit staggering to consider that with His own complex life to manage and death to endure, we were in His heart and on His mind.

Consider for a moment all the non-Christians that you know. How about those that you know well, like family, friends, coworkers, or neighbors? What about extended family, former

---

a John 17:20

friends, and people you run into at school, your kids' sports league, or the store? Various sociologists tell us that the average person interacts with upwards of a few thousand people a year. Are you praying for any of them to become Christians?

Not only does Jesus model for us the importance of praying for lost people, but He also prays for us to talk to lost people about Him as they come to "believe in me," Jesus says, "through their word."[b] Jesus alone saves people, but you and I are sent to speak to people about Him. God not only oversees the ends of things (who is saved) but also the means (how they are saved). Paul says something similar,

> For "everyone who calls on the name of the Lord will be saved." How then will they call on him in whom they have not believed? And how are they to believe in him of whom they have never heard? And how are they to hear without someone preaching? And how are they to preach unless they are sent? As it is written, "How beautiful are the feet of those who preach the good news!"
>
> —ROMANS 10:13–15

In the ancient world, a king who had an important message to deliver would have a herald run throughout the streets to declare the good news of the king. Today, we are the heralds for King Jesus, declaring that His kingdom is coming.

For this reason, not only does Jesus pray for people to become Christians, but He also prays for Christians to speak to non-Christians. Likewise, every Christian should, out of love, have a list of people they know and pray will become Christians. By praying for them, we are asking God the Holy Spirit to prepare them to hear about Jesus and prepare us to speak with them about Jesus.

---

b John 17:20

When we don't pray for people, our hearts can become cold toward them, or even angry with them. When we don't pray for people, our hearts can become filled with fear or even cowardice, which prevents us from doing the most loving thing and sharing Jesus' love with people who desperately need Him. Many non-Christians have relationships with Christians, but the subject of Jesus rarely comes up because the Christian is fearful, timid, or concerned more about personal rejection than a person's salvation.

One of the easiest ways to begin warming people up to Jesus is by simply telling them you care and asking them whether there is anyone or anything you can be praying about for them. Most of the time, even a non-Christian appreciates someone regularly praying for their need, and this opens the door of an ongoing conversation about how they are doing and how you can lovingly support them. Eventually these relationships that start with praying for someone will transition to conversations with them about Jesus.

I (Ashley) saw this point illustrated time and time again at the prayer tent. People at the university, especially those who worked there, would ask what it was all about, so I would explain the basic purpose of prayer and relationship with Jesus and ask them whether they wanted prayer for anything. Sometimes they would mention a specific request, and sometimes they wouldn't, but either way, I would kindly ask whether I could pray for them before they walked away. Of the dozens of people I offered to pray for, I only remember a handful saying no; most felt as if God gave me something to say to them that they had needed to hear, and many returned to the tent or said hi when I ran into them again. I experience the same response when I'm reading my Bible in coffee shops, blasting Christian music in my car, and countless other times that seem normal to me but cause people to stop and ask. God is always with us, so whether you are in a place that is designated for prayer or not, He will most likely cross your path with someone who needs prayer as evangelism.

JESUS PRAYS FOR OUR UNITY

God is a Father. God's people are His family. Just as Grace and I (Mark) and every parent wants their kids to love one another, forgive one another, and serve one another in unity, so God is heartbroken when division and fighting separate His kids. To make matters worse, when God's people fight and divide, we can easily forget that non-Christians are watching, and it is tough to invite them to accept Jesus and join the family that beats one another up.

As Jesus' greatest suffering has begun, it is amazing to see the last thing on His heart in His longest prayer: that the family of God would be unified and work together to see more people adopted into that family. For Jesus, our unity is His priority and the beginning of our ministry.

Read again Jesus' prayer with an emphasis on unity: "I do not ask for these only, but also for those who will believe in me through their word, that *they may all be one*, just as you, Father, are in me, and I in you, that *they also may be in us*, so that the world may believe that you have sent me. The glory that you have given me I have given to them, that *they may be one even as we are one*, I in them and you in me, that they may become *perfectly one*, so that the world may know that you sent me and loved them even as you loved me."c

Just as the Trinity is one God in three persons—Father, Son,

---

c John 17:20–23, emphasis added

194

and Spirit—so too God's people are to be one. Why? Unity is godly; division is demonic.

In God's eternal kingdom of heaven, there was only unity between God and all the divine beings (including angels, among others) until Satan created division. On the earth, there was only unity between God and our first parents until Satan again created division. After Jesus' High Priestly Prayer in John 17, the next chapter reports that Satan would again cause division, this time in Jesus' ministry leadership team, by possessing Judas to create division among the disciples and bring death to the Lord.

> Unity is godly; division is demonic.

When there is singular headship and plural leadership, there can be unity around one vision rather than division. For this reason, Jesus told us that any house divided against itself cannot stand and will eventually fall.[d]

Christian unity is all over the scriptural blueprint for community. God initiated the covenant with Abraham, promising to produce "a people," not merely a personal relationship for individuals. From the twelve tribes to the twelve disciples, the Bible consistently calls us to unity with fellow believers. Jesus sent His disciples out two by two. He traveled with twelve close followers and numerous others.

The bottom line is this: it is not safe to go out into the world by yourself. Therefore, Christianity was not designed to be lived outside of community. Biblical Christianity is a team sport. So in this section of the High Priestly Prayer, Jesus is praying that the Christian church would acquire strength in numbers.

---

d Matthew 12:25; Mark 3:25

For starters, there are two things that unity is not.

First, unity is not uniformity. The only place where everyone agrees on everything is a cult, and Christianity is not a cult but rather a family. In any family, people disagree on some things but choose to discuss or even debate them without dividing over them. Why? Because relationships matter more than issues.

For this reason Christianity has always had closehanded issues and openhanded issues. Openhanded issues, for example, include Bible translation, style of worship, mode of baptism, use of spiritual gifts, specific details of how and when God created the world, etc.). Christian unity within the church and between churches is around the closehanded issues (for example, the Bible as God's Word, the Trinity, the humanity and deity of Jesus, His death and resurrection, and the need for repentance of sin and faith in Jesus alone for salvation).

Practically, this means a line is drawn between Christians and the world, and our unity comes from being on the same side of that dividing line and agreeing on the basic truths of the Christian gospel. Sadly, this prayer of Jesus has been misused and abused by something called the ecumenical movement, which seeks to unify light and darkness by combining Christian and non-Christian beliefs in the name of love, unity, and reconciliation. When this line of distinction between the lost and found is erased, we are truly not loving people, because we cannot call them to cross over that line from life to death.

The goal of Christian unity is not ultimately that Christians would get along with non-Christians, but that Christians would remain unified with Jesus to bring non-Christians into a relationship with Jesus. If someone is lost, the most loving thing to do is invite them to cross the line of faith and be found rather than you crossing the line in their direction so that you are both lost.

To make this very clear, Christians should pray *for* Muslims, Wiccans, Hindus, Buddhists, New Agers, and people from other religions and spiritualities just as Jesus did in His prayer. Christians, however, should not pray or worship *with* people from other religions. This is actually not Christian unity because it is not unity around Christ.

When praying with someone or receiving prayer from them, it is important to verify that they are praying to the one true God! I (Ashley) can't remember the first time I prayed. It has simply always been a part of my life. But for my dad and many others, *prayer* is a word with certain connotations from bad religious experiences or pagan traditions. Things such as meditation and positive thoughts are not the same as Christian prayer, but if you don't clarify what you mean by prayer when talking to non-Christians, they will often put it in the same category. Or if someone offers to pray for you but worships a different God, you could be inviting unholy spirits.

In the name of unity the ecumenical movement tolerates false teaching. In a bizarre form of selective appropriation, they read the portion of Jesus' prayer about unity but overlook the part where He said that we should be sanctified (holy) and guided by God's Word. Subsequently it was not uncommon for them to tolerate seemingly every form of false teaching in the name of tolerance and diversity, amazingly excluding some of the clear teachings of God's Word.

Christian unity requires that we not just do good deeds to help prevent suffering in this life, but also preach the good news to help prevent suffering in eternal life. If we truly care about reducing human suffering, we cannot overlook the worst suffering of all, which is enduring the wrath of God forever in hell. For people to cross from death to life, they need to know that they are spiritually dead and need Jesus, who is the way, the truth, and the life.

Second, unity is not organizational; it is relational. Different families and churches do things differently because God usually gives us the same principles but not methods. For example:

- We are told to sing songs to the Lord but not told which songs.

- We are told to preach the Word but not told how to preach it or how long to preach it.

- We are told not to forsake regularly gathering together, but we are not told exactly when, where, or how to do this.

- We are told to train up our children but not told what that education should look like exactly.

God gives us principles in His Word and allows the Holy Spirit, guided by wisdom and conscience, to decide what our methods might be. This approach allows us to have Christian unity around our relationship with Jesus and one another, without everyone demanding one method for everyone to abide by. Practically, this means that our relational unity between Christians and churches allows great diversity in how we organize our lives, families, and churches. We see this in the Trinity, where the Father, Son, and Spirit are distinct but still unified as one God.

Some churches, denominations, networks, and ministries do not see many people come to faith in Jesus Christ because they lack unity. Internally, there is division over who the leader is, what the mission is, and what the openhanded and close-handed issues are. Externally there is division, or a lack of unity, with other Christian churches and ministries so that they are not working together as one big unified group for Team Jesus. Instead, some Christian churches and ministries sadly ignore or criticize one another rather than loving, learning, and leaning into the mission of reaching lost people together.

Jesus prays for evangelism and unity because unity provides the power for mission. When a group of people unifies around a mission, willing to pay the price to complete it and stick together, big things can happen.

This principle is true even of godless unbelievers—as in the case with the Tower of Babel, which was a demonic counterfeit to the kingdom of God. Rather than being humble and inviting God to come down to us, sinners decided to be proud and build a tower up to God. This ancient example is one of the first in a long line of demonic, works-based religions where people come together to build their version of heaven on earth without God. Seeing what was happening, "the LORD said, 'Behold, they are one people, and they have all one language, and this is only the beginning of what they will do. And nothing that they propose to do will now be impossible for them.'"[e]

Unified unbelievers are more powerful than divided believers. That is a scary truth and explains the purpose of Jesus' prayer. To end this godless unity, God then scattered the people and their languages, forcing them to be divided forever until the kingdom of God. The truth is, right now, enemies of the gospel (for example, abortion providers, transgender advocates of school curriculum, socialists, and Muslims, to name

---

e Genesis 11:6

a few) are often far more unified and far less likely to publicly divide than professing Christians.

The power of Christian unity is what Jesus meant when He said that He is the vine, and we are the branches. Only by being connected to Him and pruned by His Word can we bear fruit on our mission with Him in the world. Those who are not connected to the vine of Jesus, or those who think their tribe or team is the vine and the rest of Christianity is the branches, do not understand Jesus' prayer.

Here's one of the most important things to learn: Don't declare war on a fellow Christian. Declare allegiance to Jesus. Unity will result when we all do that.

> Unified unbelievers are more powerful than divided believers.

Where we disagree, let's open the Scriptures and learn together. Even if we cannot get to uniformity, we can still maintain unity if we stay close to Jesus, commit to Scripture and orthodox faith, and collectively strive to reach the lost for Jesus. This doesn't mean secondary things are not important. It just means we can work through those things best by loving one another and committing together to focus on essential, primary issues.

JESUS PRAYS FOR GLORY

We live in a world where seemingly everyone is trying to go up in some way. People want to make more money, have more power, live in a bigger house, go on a better vacation, drive a newer car, move to the next floor in their building or up the next rung at their company, and have more fame in terms of fans and followers.

Unlike the rest of us, Jesus Christ came down. For eternity

He sat on a throne, surrounded and served by divine beings, including angels; had worship songs sung to Him; lacked nothing; needed nothing; had all power, all wealth, and all authority ruling over all creation. Then He gave it all up to come down to be with us, to be like us, and to serve us.

Jesus' riches-to-rags story seems a bit odd to those of us who are hoping that our lives will be a rags-to-riches story. Jesus' journey from glory to humility and back into glory sounds to us as foolishness, which the Bible says it is to some who hear it. Theologians like to say that Jesus' glory was veiled while He was on the earth so that we saw merely a humble, poor, powerless Galilean peasant.

While that is how Jesus was during His earthly mission in humility, that is not how we will see Jesus in eternity. Sometimes praying through Jesus is hard because we tend to think of Him as He was in His past humility rather than how He now is in His present glory. Knowing this, Jesus prayed in John 17:24, "Father, I desire that they also, whom you have given me, may be with me where I am, to see my glory that you have given me because you loved me before the foundation of the world."

Today, Jesus has returned to glory, ruling and reigning as King of kings and Lord of lords, coming again to judge the living and the dead and

> Don't declare war on a fellow Christian. Declare allegiance to Jesus. Unity will result when we all do that.

establish a kingdom that will never end. When Jesus prayed for you, it was this Jesus who prayed for you. Today, it is still this Jesus that you pray through and who prays to the Father for you.

When we hear the word *glory,* it can at first seem like a bit of an outdated religious word. An academic reference source on the Bible says,

> For most, glory is associated with personal glory—the "glory days" of one's youth, days of lost innocence, boundless energy, unfettered imagination, and uncomplicated living. The Bible, however, moves beyond "glory" in the past tense to an emphasis on glory in the present and future tenses based on the possibility of a relationship with the God of glory.
>
> The word *glory* is derived from a Hebrew root that may mean "heavy," "weighty," or "numerous, severe" in a physical sense...The related term *kabod* expresses the attribute of "glory," "honor," "splendor" as a derived meaning of the primary idea of weightiness or gravity.[1]

Think of glory in terms of weightiness and majesty.

Regarding weightiness, there are people and things in our lives that matter most to us—meaning they outweigh other people and things. For the Christian, an example would be that the Bible outweighs all other books and that the relationship with your spouse outweighs all other human relationships.

Regarding majesty, something in us as created beings feels a sense of worshipful awe when we are in the presence of something far bigger and stronger than we are. For example, where we live in the desert of Arizona, when monsoon seasons arrive, massive clouds roll in, rain pours from the sky, and lightning lights up the night. The power and strength of a monsoon cause people to stop what they are doing and stand in awe at its power. Similarly, a few hours' drive north of us is the Grand Canyon. People from around the world travel to see what is basically a very large hole in the ground. Why? When you stand or sit on the edge, you feel incredibly small and insig-nificant—something surprisingly satisfying to the soul made for the glory of God's presence.

I (Ashley) love hiking, biking, road trips, and traveling just for this reason. Recently, after a long hiatus from traveling, my husband and I were on a road trip in northern Arizona. We live in the middle of Phoenix, surrounded by highways, skyscrapers, and manmade structures. The change in scenery from physical claustrophobia in the city to the wide-open skies of grassland put my heart back in place. I can start to feel pretty big and prideful and important when I physically can't see very far and have a limited view of the rest of the world. But when we were driving our little car down a little road in the middle of a huge open plain, I realized that it's pretty amazing that God cares about us, a very small aspect of the huge world He created.

The concept of God's glory explains one of the most popular theological phrases in the history of Christianity. One dic-tionary of theological terms speaks of *soli Deo gloria*, saying it is "a Latin phrase meaning 'to the glory of God alone.' It is one of the famous solas that express the biblical exposi-tion of the gospel given by the Protestant Reformers and their successors. (The others are sola fide [faith alone], sola gratia [grace alone], sola Scriptura [Scripture alone], and solo Christo [Christ alone].) The significance of the phrase is twofold: first, that God's supreme end in planning, purchasing, and applying salvation is His glory (Ps. 106:8; Isa. 43:25; 48:11; Ezek. 36:22; Eph. 1:6); second, that therefore the chief end and intention of those who have received God's saving grace in Christ is to bring glory to Him (1 Cor. 10:31; Rev. 4:11)."[2]

Jesus prayed that we would see Him in glory. When all is said and done and we are together forever, His prayer will be answered forever and ever. In the meantime, we live for God's glory until we see the God of glory. Jesus' prayer reminds us of four great truths about glory:

1. Our God is glorious. More powerful, wonderful, joyful, helpful, and incredible is our God than anyone or anything, or everyone and everything!

2. Our message is glorious. To have the great honor of telling people about the glorious love and grace of our great God and Savior, Jesus Christ, is an incredible honor. In a world filled with gory bad news, we get to tell people the good news of Jesus' glory!

3. Our mission is glorious. No matter where we go or what we do, the underlying mission is always the same for the Christian—to bring glory to God because God is glorious and alone worthy of glory. The Christian who eats their meal, washes their dishes, changes their baby, works their job, suffers their grief, forgives their enemy, and evangelizes their neighbor does it all to God's glory, which is the source of our joy!

4. Our future is glorious. One day there will be no more politicians or elections, tears or fears, or fights or funerals. One day everyone and every- thing that belongs to Jesus will be together in glory, forever healed, unified, and glorified with Jesus forever.

Jesus' prayer that we will see Him in glory will be fulfilled when we are glorified by Him, along with all God's people, together forever. If you belong to Jesus Christ, what God has planned for you is not only more glorious than you think; it is more glorious than you *can* think. "What no eye has seen, nor ear heard, nor the heart of man imagined, what God has prepared for those who love him."[f] Not only did Jesus pray for you to see His glory, but He also has a plan for you to share in His glory.

> In the beginning, God made humans to image him, to be like him, to dwell with him. He made us like his heavenly imagers and came to earth to unite his families, elevating humanity to share in divine life in a new world.... Scripture is clear that immortality as a divinized human is the destiny of the believer, and that our present lives in Christ are a process of becoming what we are.[3]

After Jesus wins the war to end all wars, Satan's family (angelic and human) will be sentenced to their eternal prison of hell. The two realms will be reunited, and God's two families reconciled forever. You will not be an angel or God, but you will be over the angels and more like God than you are today.

Forever you will be like Jesus Christ. "Beloved, we are God's children now, and what we will be has not yet appeared; but we know that when he appears we shall be like him, because we shall see him as he is. And everyone who thus hopes in him purifies himself as he is pure."[g] Today is the time between the times when "our citizenship is in heaven, and from it we await a Savior, the Lord Jesus Christ, who will transform our lowly body to be like his glorious body."[h]

---

f 1 Corinthians 2:9
g 1 John 3:2–3
h Philippians 3:20–21

Admittedly, this is a mystery, as the Bible is revealing a future state for you that is yet unrealized. As you await the future God has planned for you, "only let us hold true to what we have attained."[i]

Today you are "a little lower than the heavenly beings" in God's order of authority.[j] However, when God is finished with glorifying you on the other side of the second coming, you will be in authority and "judge angels."[k] Your status will change eternally and include "authority over the nations" as you rule under God.[l] Jesus' glory is something you will not only see in an unlimited sense but also share in a limited sense.

JESUS PRAYS FOR OUR DESTINY

As we close our study of Jesus' High Priestly Prayer, we see Jesus Christ our Lord, whom the Book of Hebrews calls "the radiance of God's glory," at work on the battlefield of eternity. That is how grand the scope of salvation is. That is what Jesus' High Priestly Prayer is encompassing. In this concluding section, this blessed benediction, Jesus stands in the gap between us and the Father, a gap as wide as eternity. He prays that we would be brought near the Father, even as the Father's glory is brought to bear upon the entirety of creation.

Habakkuk 2:14 tells us that one day "the earth will be filled with the knowledge of the glory of the LORD, as the waters cover the sea." Every nook and cranny of the universe will one day be set to rights, restored to the glory it reflected before the Fall. One day every square inch of the universe, over which Jesus is declaring "Mine!" on behalf of our triune God, will

i Philippians 3:16
j Psalm 8:5
k 1 Corinthians 6:3
l Revelation 2:26

radiate the fulfillment of the gospel promise: God will and has ransomed His people. God so loved the world that He sent His Son into the world—not to condemn it but that those who believe may have life eternally.[m]

Those "last days" began the day Jesus was born, quickened in pace when Jesus prayed this prayer, and opened up the flood-gates of heaven when the next day, Jesus went to the cross before bursting back from the dead three days later. Now, as then, Jesus is making God's name known through all the earth. And our mandate is to follow Jesus' example by praying for others to be saved, giving our lives in service to God's glory, and patiently waiting until the kingdom is fully unveiled once and forever.

As Jesus prayed, He was in the battle between the kingdom of light and the counterfeit world of darkness. The battle that began in heaven, continued in Eden, and raged throughout history was culminating at the cross. Knowing He would defeat Satan and deliver sinners, Jesus prayed for you and me, as we would be proclaiming His victory and serving His ministry in the world. Knowing He was returning to heaven, Jesus reminded us that while the glory of the kingdom was our home, the enemy territory of this world was the battle-field we'd be walking through to get there. In His High Priestly Prayer, no less than eighteen times in twenty-six verses, Jesus warns us about the "world."

Everything that God creates Satan counterfeits. The world is the counterfeit of the kingdom. In the world, people are cap-tives taken in war by a brutal enemy who is bent on destroying the people God made and loves. The final words of Jesus' longest prayer—prayed before He died to defeat the world and deliver

---

m John 3:16–17

those held captive by sin and death—remind us that people are our mission, and it brings glory to God to be part of the divine rescue mission to set them free. Jesus not only prayed for you, but He also invited you to be part of the greatest rescue mission in the history of the world, made possible by His death as an answer to His prayer. God has incredibly important work for you to do, incredibly valuable people for you to love, and incredibly healing words for you to speak. Jesus will send you the Spirit to make sure that His prayers are answered through your life for His glory and your joy!

The key to finding His specific next mission for you and having the power to march into that battle is to start by praying like Jesus, who prayed for you!

REFLECTION

1. Who prayed for you to become a believer? Write about your thankfulness for this person.

2. Which non-Christians can you start praying for?

3. What is your main takeaway from this book?

NOTES

CHAPTER 1

1. Gilbert K. Chesterton, *Orthodoxy* (New York: John Lane Company, 1909), 108–109.

CHAPTER 2

1. Robert H. Stein, "Fatherhood of God," *Evangelical Dictionary of Biblical Theology*, Baker Reference Library (Grand Rapids, MI: Baker Book House, 1996), 247, https://www.biblestudytools.com/dictionaries/bakers-evangelical-dictionary/fatherhood-of-god.html.
2. William J. Petersen, *Martin Luther Had a Wife* (Wheaton, IL: Tyndale House, 1983), 75.
3. George M. Marsden, *Jonathan Edwards: A Life* (New Haven, CT: Yale University Press, 2003), 133. Quoted from John Piper and Justin Taylor, *A God Entranced Vision of All Things: The Legacy of Jonathan Edwards* (Wheaton, IL: Crossway Books, 2004), 114–115.

CHAPTER 3

1. Kenneth L. Woodward, "2000 Years of Jesus," *Newsweek*, April 4, 1999, https://www.newsweek.com/2000-years-jesus-164826.
2. William L. Lane, *The Gospel of Mark, The New International Commentary on the New Testament* (Grand Rapids, MI: William. B. Eerdmans Publishing Co., 1974), 509.
3. Augustine of Hippo, *Augustine of Hippo: Selected Writings,* ed. John Farina, trans. Mary T. Clark, *The*

Classics of Western Spirituality (Mahwah, NJ: Paulist Press, 1984), 486.

CHAPTER 4

1. Sue Bowman, "Oxen No Has-Beens When It Comes to Hard Pulling," Lancaster Farming, October 29, 2011, https://www.lancasterfarming.com/news/ northern_edition/oxen-no-has-beens-when-it-comes-to-hard-pulling/article_b79a5f8f-5d4b-578d-997a-f385095dc7c9.html#:~:text=In%20fact%2C%20 while%20a%20team,as%2012%2C000%20to%20 13%2C000%20pounds.

CHAPTER 5

1. D. Martyn Lloyd-Jones, *Studies in the Sermon on the Mount* (Grand Rapids, MI: Eerdmans, 1959), 357.
2. "From World War I to 1940," Britannica, accessed September 24, 2020, https://www.britannica.com/ technology/military-communication/From-World-War-I-to-1940.
3. Elvina M. Hall, "Jesus Paid It All," Hymnary.org, 1865, https://hymnary.org/text/i_hear_the_savior_say_thy_ strength_indee.
4. Craig Blomberg, *The New American Commentary: Matthew, vol. 22* (Nashville: Broadman & Holman Publishers, 1992), 120, https://www.google.com/books/ edition/Matthew/N7m4AwAAQBAJ?hl=en&gbpv=1.

CHAPTER 6

1. Blomberg, *The New American Commentary: Matthew, vol. 22*, 395.

2. F. D. Bruner, *The Churchbook* (Dallas: Word, 1990), 979–80, who adds that Jesus' depression "teaches at least three important truths to the church: Jesus' true humanity, his free obedience and his real courage." Quoted in Blomberg, *The New American Commentary: Matthew, vol. 22*, 395.

CHAPTER 7

1. Arthur W. Pink, *Exposition of the Gospel of John* (Grand Rapids, MI: Zondervan, 1975), 903.

2. Pink, *Exposition of the Gospel of John*, 904.

3. Pink, *Exposition of the Gospel of John*, 904.

4. Pink, *Exposition of the Gospel of John*, 905.

5. Andreas J. Köstenberger, *John, Baker Exegetical Commentary on the New Testament* (Grand Rapids, MI: Baker Academic, 2004), 482.

6. "Winston Churchill Quotes," BrainyQuote, accessed September 23, 2020, https://www.brainyquote.com/quotes/winston_churchill_103788.

7. Rodney A. Whitacre, *John*, The IVP New Testament Commentary Series (Downers Grove, IL: InterVarsity Press, 1999), https://www.biblegateway.com/resources/ivp-nt/Jesus-Prays-Glorification-Father-Son.

8. Whitacre, *John*.

CHAPTER 8

1. Gerald L. Borchert, *John 12–21, vol. 25B, The New American Commentary* (Nashville: Broadman & Holman Publishers, 2002), 203–204.

2. Borchert, *John 12–21*, 203.

CHAPTER 9

1. Eugene E. Carpenter and Philip W. Comfort, *Holman Treasury of Key Bible Words: 200 Greek and 200 Hebrew Words Defined and Explained* (Nashville: Broadman & Holman Publishers, 2000), 72.

2. Alan Cairns, *Dictionary of Theological Terms* (Greenville, SC: Emerald House Group, 2002), 425.

3. Michael S. Heiser, *The Unseen Realm: Recovering the Supernatural Worldview of the Bible* (Bellingham, WA: Lexham Press, 2015), 319–320.

My **<u>FREE GIFT</u>** to You

Dear Reader,

We hope *Pray Like Jesus* didn't change just your prayer life but your *entire life*. As a thank-you, we are offering you the e-book for *Win Your War* for **FREE!**

To get your **FREE GIFT**, please go to:

www.DriscollBooks.com/gift

God bless,

Pastor Mark Driscoll

Ashley Chase

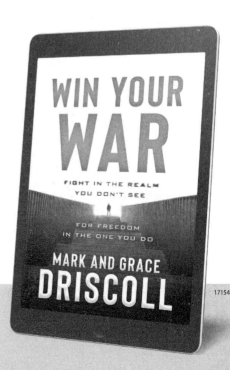

To **DEEPEN YOUR STUDY** and practice of prayer, check out our *Pray Like Jesus* YouVersion plan!

With more than ninety thousand completions, *Pray Like Jesus* is a twenty-one-day Bible-led journey designed to take the mystery and monotony out of prayer. You will learn from Jesus' teaching about prayer as well as His own prayer life. *Pray Like Jesus* explores what prayer is, whom we pray to, how we should pray, what we should pray for, and when and where we should pray.

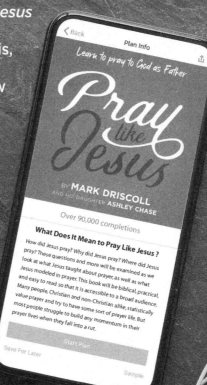

YouVersion Bible App